KAFKA
AND
PRAGUE

KAFKA AND PRAGUE

Text by Johann Bauer
Photographs by Isidor Pollak
Design by
Jaroslav Schneider
Translated by P. S. Falla

PRAEGER PUBLISHERS
New York · Washington · London

Published in the United States of America in 1971

Praeger Publishers, Inc.
111 Fourth Avenue, New York, N.Y. 10003, U.S.A.
5 Cromwell Place, London SW 7, England

Published in German as *Kafka und Prag*
© 1971 by Chr. Belser Verlag, Stuttgart, Germany
Translation © 1971 by Pall Mall Press Limited

Library of Congress Catalog Card Number: 73–153833

Printed in Germany by Chr. Belser Verlag, Stuttgart

Contents

Prague does not let go — either of you or of me. This little mother has claws. There is nothing for it but to give in or—. We would have to set it on fire from two sides, at the Vysehrad and at the Hradschin, only thus could we free ourselves.

I THE POET AND HIS CITY

Are you trying to make me believe
that I am unreal, a ridiculous sight
on the green pavement?

Franz Kafka's native city of Prague lies in the heart of Europe, at a meeting-point of ancient cultures. During a history of more than a thousand years it came to represent a unique spiritual phenomenon, which found expression in the importance and variety of its cultural traditions and in the rich contrasts of its architecture. Kafka's whole life was spent in the midst of this splendid setting. His parents, who had come to Prague from different regions of the Czech countryside, took up their abode in a neighbourhood where they felt at home as Jews and where there seemed to be the best chance of making a living. This was in the centre of the Old City near the ancient ghetto, which was on the point of being swept away by a drastic clearance program. The family moved many times from one house to another, but only within a radius of a hundred yards or so from the Old City square—an area which the tourist today can easily cover between lunch and afternoon tea.

Kafka was born in a house next to the baroque church of St. Nicholas, which closes off one side of the historic square. His first steps to school would have taken him from the house alongside the Old City town hall, with its famous clock, on which a procession of the Apostles marked the hours, past the spot where twenty-seven Czech nobles were executed in 1621 after the catastrophe of the White Mountain—an event which marked Czech history for centuries to come—and then across the square and along by the Tyn church, in which Tycho Brahe lies buried. After Kafka's father became well-to-do he owned a wholesale business in the Kinsky Palace on the square; the same building housed the German Gymnasium, where Franz completed his schooling. Franz later lived successively in two houses in the elegant, rebuilt St. Nicholas Street (now Paris Street), the Art Nouveau charm of which was to delight André Breton. To get to the Workers' Insurance Office, where he worked, he would walk around the Powder Tower at the end of the Graben (Na Príkope, the former moat of the city), a favourite promenade and centre of the social life of Old Prague. In the evening, on his way to a lecture or literary reading, he would stroll along another main street full of social and cultural activity, the Ferdinandka (now National Street), which ends at the Vltava river in front of that supreme symbol of nineteenth-century Czech culture, the National Theatre.

Although the scene of Kafka's daily life was thus saturated in history, we must not draw superficial conclusions as to the relationship between it and his literary work. Kafka was less sensitive to the romance of Bohemian history than most of his Prague contemporaries. Amidst all these monuments of the past he lived and grappled with problems which to all appearances were far more trivial, ephemeral and personal. In his life and thought, the *genius loci* is not written large. It rather conjures up a picture of narrow lanes with immemorial houses and old-fashioned, crowded shops—lanes sparingly lit by gas-lamps, which the strange inhabitants of the Old City themselves kindled at nightfall; alleys whose mysterious charm was at its strongest in the morning, when they awoke to a rather shoddy commercial activity, and at night in the bluish glow of the lamps, when the solitary wanderer listened, half-alarmed, to the echo of his own footsteps. The tangle of alleyways and houses with double entrances (in German *Durchhäuser*), in which only a native of the capital 'baptized with Vltava water' could find his way; the gloomy magnificence of spacious old courtyards and dwellings, that aroused Ilya Ehrenburg's admiration many years later; the balconies on which so much of Prague's outdoor life was lived; the lofts, stairways and apartments of the Old City—all these go to create what we may, with every caution, term the 'ambience' of Kafka's work.

Throughout its history Prague has been a cultural and social melting-pot. Rulers and ruled, gentry and commoners, foreign refinement and native robustness, urban sophistication and young blood from the country—Czechs, Germans and Jews, not to mention other nationalities, lived higgledy-piggledy in a strange symbiosis. To this society, the Czech national awakening in the nineteenth century brought fresh tensions. The German-speaking community, which had hitherto borne all the marks of a social élite, was gradually smothered by the influx of racial Czechs from the countryside: it became more and more shut in on itself and succumbed to a form of degeneration marked, among other things, by extraordinary intellectual subtlety. The historically progressive, thrusting, biologically healthy Czech element stood in contrast to the German and Jewish enclave of businessmen, state officials and an increasingly rootless intelligentsia. Kafka's father Hermann had come up from the country and, as we now know, was inclined, till he arrived in Prague, to consider himself rather a Czech than a German. His decision to join the German enclave was made deliberately for economic reasons: the propertied class with their old commercial traditions were a world apart from the rustic simplicity of the Czech community. Franz Kafka duly embraced a career in the Imperial and Royal bureaucracy, the path to which was opened by a doctorate in law.

At the end of the century, when the air was already full of symptoms of the decline of the German community in Prague,

there took place an extraordinary florescence of literature in the German language. The term 'a Prague German' became almost synonymous with 'writer', a fact that became the staple of humorous anecdote. How did this passionate desire for creativity take root in the isolated, dying community, cut off from organic contact with the centres of live German speech? Perhaps it was the last and clearest symptom of that community's decline, the swan song of a society losing its hold on reality. Kafka's work makes a contribution of its own to answering this question—not that it is concerned with events of his day or the changes taking place in society. How little Kafka was concerned with world-shaking events may be judged from the entry in his Diary for August 2, 1914: 'Germany has declared war on Russia. Went to swimming class in the afternoon.' Nor does his work tell us about any specific milieu. Attempts to localize this or that episode are no more than a game for literary historians. Tourist guides will point out three or four originals of Kafka's 'Castle', each about as convincing as the other. Nor, finally, does he tell us anything about the typical human being of a specific period: exact though his descriptions are, the works are too general and too much outside time for such a purpose. In them we see the world through the imagination of someone self-restricted to a narrow cycle of indisputable everyday experiences: the picture is made up of elements of reality, but it is an imaginary picture for all that.

Today the streets of Kafka's Prague are filled with a different type of people, to whom its former German culture means nothing. Only the scenery has changed little since his time. The old monuments remain firmly anchored in time and space, though some lesser things wear a different guise. Kafka's world is most plainly to be seen in details, which the uncanny sharpness of his description enables us to recognize today: the pavement, the stones, the crumbling walls, the old house-signs, the Art Nouveau decoration at this place or that. As for his own life, there is not a great deal we can learn about it from the written word. This timid, retiring writer made little impression on the world either as a man or as a citizen. His literary activity was a struggle against impotence, a vain, never-ceasing attempt to 'break the circle' by which he had been shut in once and for all. It was an inner need, unaccompanied by any special concern to preserve what he had written; most of his works remained fragmentary, and he generally spoke slightingly of them. Rivalry and the pride of authorship were foreign to him. He took no interest in the literary world, and scarcely knew any authors personally. His writing was part and parcel of a desperate, life-and-death struggle; he had no wish that it should survive him. The result of his indifference was that Max Brod, who went through his papers after his death and collected a chaotic pile of manuscripts, found himself one of the most fortunate owners in literary history.

Kafka was little known while he was alive, and nothing was heard of him for years after his death. Then came the period of discovery, appreciation and publication of his works, the interpretation of which became one of the most popular literary puzzles of the twentieth century. At one time there would be a craze for them, at another they would be regarded as an awful warning. An author who, ten years after his death, was still known only to a narrow circle of friends and relations suddenly became the most frequently studied phenomenon in modern literature. As many works have been written about him in latter years as about Dante, Cervantes, Shakespeare or Goethe. Students of German literature who would once have written degree theses about Goethe now write them about Kafka. From Brod's monograph onwards, the first works of substance began to appear some ten years after his death, a lapse of time which has left unfortunate gaps in our knowledge. The extent of our ignorance about his life and the location or publication of some manuscripts is such that for many years past every new fact has been hailed as an important discovery.

All roads to Kafka lead through Prague. Unfortunately, for various reasons the task of systematic investigation was left till too late, and we know too little about Kafka's family, his professional and university life, the cultural milieu in which he moved and the people he came in contact with. When Klaus Wagenbach, his first critical biographer, came to Prague in the middle fifties he found many scattered documents to which no one had paid attention, and many people who knew all sorts of things but had never been questioned. It became clear by degrees that the gaps in our knowledge might be filled by an infinity of painstaking work, the difficulty of which was lessened by the close affinity between Kafka's writings and his personality. Kafka is an author one does not get tired of: his work remains lively not only by reason of its artistic merit but also thanks to its inexhaustible meaning.

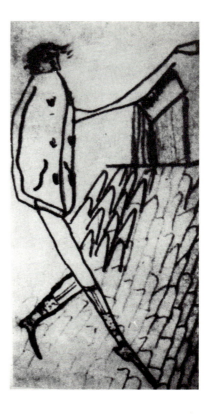

In the early sixties a fresh lot of papers was found in Prague: a bundle of family letters, including a series addressed to Kafka's youngest sister Ottla. Two years ago the present author succeeded in tracing a quantity of official documents concerning him, mostly from police archives, and it is quite probable

that more will come to light. The ground is mapped out in such a way that we now know where to look. Even if only a speck of gold is discovered in a mountain of sand, its value more than repays the effort of research.

Basic research has now become all the more necessary because studies of Kafka, including far-reaching interpretations strongly coloured by the philosophical approach of their authors, have expanded to such vast dimensions. It is time to return to primary sources, and clearly Prague is still the best place for further investigation. A detailed examination of sources will enable us to give a fuller picture of Kafka's years at the German University and in the Workers' Insurance Office, and will confirm or rebut the supposition that he was in contact with Czech anarchist groups. It will also make it possible to explain more fully his relations with the Czech community and the influence of his work on Czech culture.

The present work analyzes for the first time the new material on Kafka from the Prague archives, especially the police dossier and other documents illustrating his contacts with the authorities in numerous fields. Everyone knows what the world of bureaucracy signified to Kafka, and what a part it plays in his work. The documents now brought to light have something thoroughly Kafkaesque about them, in their style of writing and pedantic arrangement and in their perfect system of cross-references. We may indeed thank the Imperial and Royal bureaucracy for facilitating our work and enabling us, like the boy in the fairy tale, to trace a whole kingdom once we have found a single sheep. The subject matter of the documents is no less Kafkaesque than their form: for instance the elaborate petitions, couched in polished rhetoric, for 'favours' on the part of officialdom which, to our way of thinking, are simple matters of course. Or the circumstances in which, at the very end of the war, Kafka almost received a decoration for organizing a sanatorium for ex-servicemen; or again the fact that, ten years after his death, the military authorities were still trying to track him down in order to issue his certificate of discharge. All these things, of no great importance in themselves, are of peculiar interest in relation to the very personal fate of Franz Kafka. We must not underrate the importance of official documents to one whose whole life was a struggle with forms, a kind of interminable lawsuit.

The object of this work is to approach the study of Kafka from the viewpoint of ascertainable facts. This is not intended to conflict in any way—nor can it do so—with an interpretative approach, which, though radically different, is equally justified.

Respect for concrete facts, texts and documents is a useful corrective to abstractions of all kinds, which by their nature tend to depart from the facts and may, as a result, conflict with one another. The choice of viewpoint is emphasized by the illustrations, especially those that reproduce with precision authentic details.

To our generation Kafka has become—in a different way for each individual—the formulator of great problems, a prophet and philosopher, a miraculous anticipator of historical and literary developments. Each reader is inclined to generalize the meaning of the text, down to its most casual statements and metaphors. Over the widest possible field, we find emphasized again and again the affinity between Kafka's world and the grotesque, mysterious menace of events in our own lives, or the chaos which modern civilization is inflicting in the name of rationalism. This approach to his work may be unwelcome to specialists who, having discovered its actual sources, are concerned as far as possible to interpret the result in concrete historical terms. Nevertheless it testifies to the scope and intensity of Kafka's writings, their symbolic force and the power that emanates from them. For, as we have seen, the real-life basis of his works is extremely narrow. An untypical, ill-balanced personality, incredibly complicated and prone to self-contradiction, he lived in the restricted circle of his family and a few friends, in a tiny quarter of his native city and in a few other places which he visited as a stranger, making no impression on them and receiving none. He was a stranger, too, in the literary world of his time: few of its members had heard of him, and he took from it only the modicum that he really needed. His greatness, therefore, is not that of an all-embracing panorama. It rests on a small base, on a narrow, closed circle; but his experiences are given shape with a degree of literary intensity and penetration that we do not find in writers either before or after him.

II ORIGINS

The house in which Kafka was born, in the Altstädter Ring (Staroměstské náměstí) on the edge of the Jewish quarter. It was built by Dientzenhofer as a clergy house for St. Nicholas's church.

Franz Kafka's childhood and early youth were spent uninterruptedly in Prague, but his parents were comparative newcomers to the city. His father Hermann came from the village of Osek (German Wossek) near Strakonice in southwest Bohemia, while his mother Julie, née Löwy, was from the town of Podebrady some 30 miles east of Prague. Ever since the latter part of the eighteenth century there had been a migration to Prague from the Czech and Moravian countryside, which did much to further the Czech national renaissance in the cultural and political capital of Bohemia. The influx of new blood, of Czech speakers who felt themselves to be Czechs, was a basis for the development of the national movement in Prague, a city of age-long international tradition in the field of culture, in which the German-Jewish minority had almost monopolized the spheres of bureaucracy, commerce and high finance. At the same time, citizens of Jewish faith like Kafka's parents also migrated to Prague, as a natural consequence of the emancipation of country-dwelling Jews after 1860.

The Austrian constitution promulgated after the revolution of 1848 ended a long chapter in the history of state anti-Semitism. After centuries of harsh discrimination the Jews had in fact begun to enjoy basic liberties in 1781 —exactly a hundred years before Hermann Kafka's arrival in Prague—when the emperor Joseph II began to issue a series of decrees designed to solve the Jewish question in the light of rationalist principles. The Jews were no longer compelled to wear conspicuous yellow badges of racial infamy; they were allowed to learn crafts and pursue higher studies—the first Jewish doctor in Austria took his degree in 1788, the first lawyer in 1790—to own land and to serve in the army. They were also allowed to practise their religion freely and to leave the ghetto. In Prague it was naturally the richer Jews who took advantage of this privilege and moved to the newer quarters of the city.

However, the Josephine reforms did not confer full equality on the Jewish community, and in some ways they made its position worse. Strict Germanization prevailed in education and in other spheres: every Jew had to adopt a German surname, and Jewish businessmen had to keep their books in German, so that no one could make a living without a knowledge of the language. Finally, a *numerus clausus* was imposed on the number of Jewish families in the country as a whole and in individual towns: the right to found a family was confined to the first-born son in each generation, known as the *familiant*. A Jew, for instance, could only move to Prague with his family when a 'place' fell vacant, and provided he met the property qualification.

Jewish emancipation in the Austrian dominions was completed early in the reign of the emperor Franz Joseph, when the 1848 constitution removed the disabilities that had not been done away with by Joseph II. It proclaimed the equality of all religious denominations, and in 1860—when both Kafka's parents were still children—Jews became fully equal with other races and nationalities in the eyes of the law. The Prague ghetto had virtually ceased to exist: in 1850 it was incorporated with the rest of the city under the name of Josefstadt, in memory of the liberal emperor. At that time there were 8,500 Jews in Prague, as against a Christian population of 115,000. After 1860, when the more prosperous Jews had long since left the ghetto, it became a refuge for impoverished Christians as well as Jews; it was rapidly becoming a slum, but was less thickly populated than before. It was here that Hermann Kafka first fixed his abode when he arrived in Prague from south Bohemia.

Ignát Herrmann, the well-known Czech writer and authority on old Prague, has given a vivid description of the Fifth District of those days, known familiarly as '*bei den Juden*':

'... The whole place gave the impression that the rules of the outside world were in abeyance, and that a solitary traveller was exposed to the mercy of other powers—invisible, mysterious and hostile.

'The streets were covered with filth and refuse; children ran about half-naked, and in front of the houses half-naked women performed intimate household tasks or sat about gossiping at the end of the day, having finished work and perhaps gone for an evening stroll.

'In many streets, house after house was a brothel... On the ground floor of one, the customers might be offered weak,

over-stewed coffee or at best lemonade, while on the first floor of the next-door house they could drink champagne to their heart's content.

'Behind the heavy, huddled walls of the Fifth District, what a fantastic mixture there was of riotous living and strict Jewish orthodoxy! Cheek by jowl with the haunts of vice and debauchery were the austere houses of believing Jews who locked their doors at nightfall, kept the Sabbath, and observed the high festivals in traditional style. While the taverns and coffee-houses rang with the crazy mirth of Saturday-night revellers, the synagogues and other houses of prayer, of which there were some forty in the Jewish quarter of Prague, would be filled with the monotonous chant of their congregations.'

Emancipation had important social and ethical consequences for the Jews. Freedom of movement led to the breaking up of enclaves; it put an end to their isolation amongst the peasantry and tended to dissolve the internal ties which had been charac-

Franz's mother Julie, née Löwy, the daughter of a well-to-do Prague bourgeois family.

teristic of Jewish groups. The disintegration affected all aspects of life, from religious orthodoxy to everyday customs. The sense of their own past, the atmosphere of the ghetto as a spiritual and physical expression of the diaspora began to seem, to most Jews, something unfamiliar and mysterious, instinct with a strange magic like a voice from the bowels of the earth. Franz Kafka himself is a striking example of this. Having set

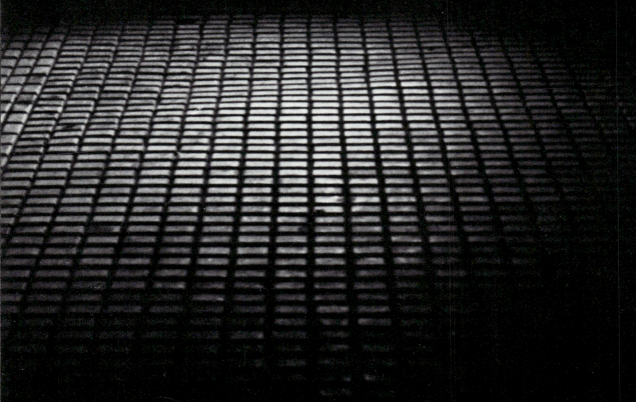

out with the motto, inherited from his father, of '*Nichts vom Judentum*', he later spent many years patiently and laboriously rediscovering his 'faith' in Jewishness.

Hermann Kafka's own father was a country butcher who, being a second son, did not acquire the right to found a family until 1848, when he was 35 years old; he then wasted no time in marrying a neighbour's daughter. Their son Hermann had a hard time in his youth: he had to work from a tender age, carting goods about the countryside in the depth of winter, in clothes that failed to keep him warm. In later life he made these hardships a source of permanent reproach to his own children, who certainly had nothing of the kind to suffer. This attitude is characteristic of his whole behaviour towards Franz in particular. Another decisive factor was the father's robustness, practical sense and love of hard work, while the memory of his early sufferings imbued him with admiration for everything to do with success, efficiency, enterprise and social advancement. For this reason he was glad to leave his native village, where he had endured so much humiliation and where, as a Jew, he could not hope for much of a future; and for the same reason, although in language and otherwise he was more a Czech than a German, when he moved to Prague he attached himself to the German community and resolved that his children should be brought up as Germans. He chose as his commercial emblem, however, as a real German would hardly have done, a jackdaw perching on a branch, in allusion to the meaning of his name in Czech (*kavka*).

Hermann Kafka's career and his ability to cope with life gave his son a sense of inferiority. At every turn, the highly strung Franz felt the enormous distance between his own world and his father's, with its robust, rustic background. While the latter's energy was channelled into commercial enterprise and achievement, Franz's was expended on what must have seemed the more and more unreal accomplishment of writing. The upshot was a deep and lasting misunderstanding between father and son.

As to Franz's mother, she brought to the marriage and to the home an inheritance of kindness, tenderness and Rabbinical wisdom which at times, according to her brothers, verged on whim and eccentricity. To her fell the role of a perpetual peacemaker, smoothing over the antagonisms that arose day by day.

These two very different characters—the husband strong, self-confident and masterful, the wife gentle, sensitive and fair-minded—met soon after Hermann Kafka had come to Prague.

Kafka's father Hermann (or Herrmann) was the son of a butcher, Jakob Kafka, in the village of Wossek in southern Bohemia.

Pages 24 and 25: left, the entrance hall and front door of the house in which Kafka was born.

Right: the next-door house 'The Green Frog'.

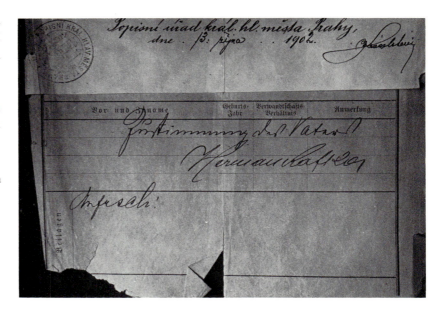

You had worked your way right up by your own efforts, and as a result you had absolute faith in your own opinion. This was less overwhelming to me as a child than when I became a growing youth. You sat in your armchair, and from there you governed the world. Your opinion was the right one and all the others were daft, crazy, senseless, abnormal. Such was your self-confidence that you could be full of inconsistency without ever ceasing to be right.

He was living at that time in the squalor of the Judenstadt, while Julie's home was in an old mansion on the Altstädter Ring (the Old Town square). Their first married home, where Franz, the eldest child, was born, was alongside St. Nicholas's church, close to the square and on the edge of the former ghetto: in those days it bore the number 27. The house, which was spacious but dilapidated, had been the abode of the Slavonic Benedictines until the order was dissolved in 1787. It then passed into private hands, and from 1816 to 1866 was used as a German theatre and opera-house. Later the once handsome monastery buildings were turned into shops of various kinds or leased to impoverished tenants, among whom we must count the Kafkas at the outset of their life in Prague. The house was a kind of projection of the ghetto, and their stay in it, which lasted less than two years, indicates their limited means and Hermann's social level at the beginning of his business career. It was one of the first buildings to be demolished in the 'clearance' of the ghetto in 1897. A new house, numbered 24/1, was erected in 1903 on the site of the former abbot's residence; it has a similar façade, with one more storey, but the ground plan is different. The stone gateway and balcony of the old building were incorporated into the new. Biographies of Kafka generally state incorrectly that he was born in the house known as 'U veze' (Beside the Tower).

The clearance of the ghetto was decreed by Ordinance No. 22 of January 11, 1893 and carried out from 1897 to 1917; but it had been gradually prepared for a whole decade previously, and thus took place literally before Franz Kafka's eyes. As with many other important events that occurred in his lifetime, there is scarcely a word about it in his writings, but he must

surely have been affected by such a radical change in the surroundings among which he grew up. Gustav Janouch, a Prague writer, has recorded Kafka's comment in the following words: 'They are all still alive in us—the dark corners, the mysterious alleys, the sightless windows, dirty courtyards, noisy pothouses and secretive inns. We walk about the broad streets of the new town, but our steps and looks are uncertain; we tremble inwardly as we used to do in the old miserable alleyways. Our hearts know nothing yet of any clearance: the insanitary old ghetto is much more real than our new, hygienic surroundings. We walk about as in a dream, and we ourselves are only a ghost of former times.'

The transformation of the Jewish quarter was the most drastic and significant operation of its kind in the history of Prague. A sordid, tumbledown, socially degraded area which had long ceased to serve its original purpose, and which attracted from a distance but repelled at close quarters, was all at once converted into one of the 'smartest' parts of the capital. We can see clearly enough now that the conception was not a happy one: an architectural complex which would today be unique in Europe was replaced by the questionable splendour of *fin de siècle* promoterism. The effect was to ruin the skyline of the Old City, whose main features, including the monuments of the Jewish past, were submerged in a sea of tenements. The centre of Prague was invaded by the architecture of the suburbs, and there was no attempt to solve the problem of linking the new buildings with the historic ones that remained.

In any case, a district of striking poverty was turned into an elegant commercial quarter. It may seem strange, but it is characteristic of the Jewish community in the Old City, that Hermann Kafka, who moved house so many times, only once in his life—and that for five months—lived anywhere except in the neighbourhood of the Old City and the former ghetto. As for Franz, who lived with his parents for three-quarters of his life, there was never a time when he was not surrounded by concrete memories of the past. There was the Altstädter Ring near the Moldau (Vltava) with its ancient fording-place, the very heart of Prague from the earliest times. Apart from the old square and the Grosser and Kleiner Ring with their historic buildings, the area is dominated by the church of Our Lady of Tyn with the nearby 'Ungelt' (staple or tolbooth), where foreign merchants unpacked their wares and paid excise duty as long ago as the tenth century. Further on is St. Nicholas's, the principal church of the Old City until the end of the fourteenth century; beyond it the Judenstadt with its synagogues, town

Pages 28/29: balconies overlooking the courtyard in the house where Kafka was born.
Right: the house across the street from it.

A house with entrances in two streets (*Durchhaus*) and an alley near the Alt-städter Ring.

hall and cemetery. Off the square are Melantrich Street, the Eisengasse (Zelezná) with the ancient Charles University (Caro-linum) where Kafka attended lectures; then the Zeltnergasse (Celetná) leading to the Powder Tower and on to the Por-schitscherstrasse (Poríc), his daily route to the insurance office. Or the Lange Gasse (Dlouhá trída), where he sat in the 'Golden Pike' planning his life with Felice Bauer, or Paris Street (Parízská), the most elegant in the rebuilt quarter, in which he lived at three different addresses in the course of his life. Places like these, where every stone has its history and every house is full of memories, make a profound impression even on casual visitors. Anyone who lives there for long, as Kafka did, must be enthralled by their charm and mystery. Kafka is said to have made the characteristic remark: 'We Jews are old from the moment we come into the world.' In a complex way, his works reflect a deep sense of the geography and history of old Prague. Their factual basis may seem to us extremely minute, more so than with almost any other twentieth-century author; but the whole of his material enters fully into the composition of his images. Every description, however precise and detailed, is a fantasy created out of real elements. It is typical of him that the only specific description of historic Prague that appears in his works is in the Diary, where it figures as part of the record of a dream. The scene is a theatre, and Kafka is sitting in the gallery:

'In one act the scenery was so enormous that nothing else was visible—neither the stage, nor the footlights, nor the darkened auditorium. In fact, the whole audience was itself on the stage, and the scene was that of the Altstädter Ring, probably seen from the corner of the Niklasstrasse. In real life this would have meant that one could not see the part of the square in front of the Rathaus clock, or the Kleiner Ring; but in my dream the stage shifted from time to time in such a way that, for instance, one could see the view of the Kleiner Ring from the Kinsky Palace. The only purpose of this was to display the scene as a whole—it was in fact there in all its perfection and it would have been a thousand pities to leave out any of it, since, as I well knew, it is the most beautiful setting that has ever been seen on earth. The sky was overcast with dark, autumnal clouds; an occasional flash of sunlight was reflected from a coloured window-pane in the southeast corner of the square. Everything was life-size and in perfect detail: it was curious to see windows being blown open and shut by the breeze, sound-lessly because the houses were so tall. The square sloped away at a sharp angle; the pavement was almost black; the Tyn church

33

was in its proper place, but in front of it stood a little Imperial
palace with a courtyard in which all the other monuments in
the square were tidily arranged: the pillar of Our Lady, the
fountain that used to be in front of the Rathaus and which I
have never seen, the other fountain in front of St. Nicholas's
and the wooden fence around the site that is being excavated
for the Huss monument.'

This, with its geographical precision, is an evocative description of what Kafka calls 'the most beautiful setting that has
ever been seen on earth'. Yet the great changes that accompanied the clearance of the ghetto and caused such a stir among
the German and Czech communities at the time left little trace
on Kafka's work, despite the fact that so much of it consists of
'personal' material such as diaries and correspondence. His reaction to these matters was deeper, more indirect and subjective.
When a new bridge was being built across the river at the spot
where the Law Faculty now is, Kafka, viewing from his window the stump projecting over the waters, described it as a
'taking-off place for suicides'. The image throws an interesting

light on the relation in Kafka's mind between the inner and the outer world. Gradually the circle closes in on him and creates an impassable barrier, destroying his link with the world and his ability to solve the problems connected with it.

Kafka's childhood, which was of extraordinary importance in his life and to which he constantly recurs in his writings, was spent in an atmosphere of constraint. His parents were overworked; his father treated the children, and especially his first-born Franz, with unselfish but inexorable strictness; his mother strove to allay the tension caused by the father's perpetual harshness; his sisters were so much younger than Franz that they could not give him any companionship in childhood. His upbringing was mainly left to servants, particularly the cook, or to a Czech or foreign governess. All this produced in him an oppressive loneliness and a coldly fanciful outlook, and threw him into a state of uncertainty about his ability to deal with the outside world. This, no doubt, was the origin of his passivity in matters that those around him thought important, and his contrasting activity in directions that they did not approve or understand. The result was a state of constant conflict with his surroundings, especially with his father, and a feeling of anxiety, incomprehension and self-distrust. He was afraid, too, of maturity. His father's example paralyzed him, and his feeling of inadequacy grew, as time went on, into a sense of complete uncertainty and of the incomprehensibility of things: that what happens in the world is not governed by logic but by fantasy, and that the absurdest events are the most normal. His father was no doubt one of the main causes of what Kafka called 'the systematic destruction of myself over a period of years', comparing it to 'the slow, remorseless development of an abdominal hernia'. The process of self-destruction was continued by Kafka himself, who, having once and for all lost his self-confidence, took his own personality as a target. As he wrote in the Diary: 'Every day at least one line must be aimed at myself, in the same way as people are now aiming their telescopes at the comet.' Thus, at the time of Halley's comet, he was using his writing as a tool of self-destruction. This meant that from his youth onwards he took a rigorous view of life, concentrating on the problem of his own existence and endlessly dissecting the simplest actions and attitudes vis à vis his parents and relatives, teachers and superiors.

His school life did not suffice to counteract the family influence or cure him of growing self-distrust, fear and uncertainty; nor, on the other hand, does it seem to have satisfied his strongly developing imagination.

III CHILDHOOD AND YOUTH

The Kinsky Palace on the Altstädter Ring. The German Gymnasium occupied the first floor; Hermann Kafka's wholesale business was on the ground floor to the right.

The atmosphere of old Prague was not an ordinary one, and the period of Kafka's youth was fraught with human conflict. In Prague as in the rest of Bohemia, the latter part of the nineteenth century saw much social development and profoundly changing customs and values. The old monarchy had long suffered from various ills, due in large measure to the problems arising from the multiplicity of its nationalities. The Slavs in the Austrian half of the empire, especially the Czechs, had suffered from the Austro-Hungarian 'compromise' of 1867 and were agitating more and more vigorously against Austrian rule. The Czechs were in a key position, since they formed the nucleus of Austrian state-controlled industry, and the intelligentsia of the rapidly reviving nation was an increasingly important part of the political élite. They were a community which the central power was careful to confine within bounds, but they were rapidly developing a self-confidence rooted in their glorious past, and were putting forward political demands with increasing determination: their immediate purpose was to achieve greater independence within the Austrian confederation (*Staatenbund*), while the ultimate goal was the creation of a separate State. Czech nationalism, fostered by oppression and based on the vitality of the masses, expressed itself in a variety of forms in the second half of the century, from rule-of-law conservatism through progressive liberalism to social democracy, the last combining the national struggle with a more or less radical campaign for social rights.

The conflict which resulted from the age-old relationship between Czechs and Germans in Bohemia manifested itself at various levels. It was accentuated by the fact that the empire was governed on a national basis, so that German and Czech

Franz Kafka as a pupil at the Imperial and Royal *Staatsgymnasium* (1893).

representatives (as well as Hungarians, Southern Slavs and Ruthenians) confronted one another in parliament and public offices, education, finance and commerce, and their rivalry in all these fields was a major source of tension. The growth of the Czech population of Prague—it increased nearly four times between 1850 and 1900—led to a situation of crisis there, since the dwindling German-Jewish minority, with no natural hinterland and no base of support among the rural and working population, still held most key posts in the administration and in commercial and industrial life. In the cultural field, German-Czech relations in Bohemia developed differently. As time went on, they were increasingly marked by mutual lack of interest rather than antagonism: it should not surprise us therefore to find, at least in the higher cultural spheres, so little German-Austrian influence on Czech life at this period. The barriers between the two cultures were especially strong in the mixed, polyglot society of old Prague, where there was a marked element of official policy in their separation. Kafka's own interest in Czech matters is highly exceptional.

The national struggle took a different course again in private life, outside the sphere of institutions. From the beginning of their emancipation the Czech people's will to exist as a nation took the form of independence of everything German, particularly in the field of language, where the free development of Czech was regarded as fundamental to national and cultural progress. They also did their utmost to win back the Germanized sections of the population for the Czech cause. By the second half of the nineteenth century this battle had been won: fears for the nation's continued existence had disappeared, and self-confidence had grown to the point where it was possible to coexist more or less tranquilly with the German community. The spirit of mutual toleration was reflected in the commercial circles of old Prague, where the name-plates of firms were generally inscribed in both Czech and German. Relations began to be exacerbated as newcomers moved in, especially Germans from the provinces, most of whom were of the nationalist persuasion. It was not to be expected that two rival nationalisms, separated by language, should get along peaceably under the same roof.

Old Prague, moreover, was a Jewish city, in that most of the long-established German residents were Jews. In the course of time the Jewish community had become increasingly isolated. They were divided by language from the Czechs, who thought of them as Germans, and by almost everything else from the new Germans, who thought of them as Jews. Memories of the

Pages 40/41: a courtyard in the Kinsky Palace.
Right: the front staircase and entrance to the Gymnasium.

I often used to imagine the terrifying assembly of teachers (school is only the most straightforward example, it was the same in all other aspects of life) who, when I moved up from the first form to the second, from the second to the third and so on, would, I thought, convene and solemnly discuss the unique and outrageous fact that I, the most incapable and most ignorant of pupils, had actually managed to creep up into the next class—a class which, now that general attention was focused on me, would naturally spew me out forthwith, to the delight of the righteous who had been oppressed by this nightmare situation.

ghetto were dying out: Franz Kafka belonged to the second generation of those who lived outside it. Physically it was a thing of the past, but there was still a 'sociological ghetto', a barrier between two nations which one could only cross at the cost of one's identity. Nevertheless, the trend towards assimilation was increasingly strong. Orthodox Judaism also persisted, though the spirit of the times was against it and it was eroded from every side. Between these two there was a third path, equally precarious if not more so: that of those Jews, mainly intellectuals, whose Judaism was slipping away from them —who did not want to give it up, but could scarcely retrieve it from the past—and whose certainty based on bygone days was increasingly stifled by the uncertainty of the present. This was the category to which Franz Kafka belonged.

Prague, with its unique juxtaposition of nationalities, faiths and cultures, was an arena of conflict between the most varied elements at all stages of development: the Czechs, in the dawn of their national life, looking hopefully towards the future; the Germans, holding a commanding position, but lacking linguistic or biological roots and haunted by fears of their own decline; and the Jews, alien to both the main social groups, and groping between an outworn faith and hope for better things to come. All these cross-currents and unruly elements made old Prague an incalculable city of extraordinary variety. The boundaries between different spheres were constantly changing, as languages, religions, nationalities and ways of life continued to mingle in a colourful process. It was a world in which the individual felt uncertain of himself, a period of transition in the fullest sense. Steeped in the ancient history of the city, major issues dissolved into grotesquerie, into the crazy pattern of the Prague streets, market-squares and inns. Mixtures of all kinds were typical: spoken Czech bristled with German words, and the stiffness of written German was deeply influenced by Czech in all its aspects, from syntax to phraseology. The same mixture was to be found in popular entertainment, music-halls and theatres, where audiences of all communities mingled freely. The dominant elements of this mixed culture, admirably exemplified in Hasek's 'Good Soldier Schweik', were the irrepressible humour and fantasy of the man in the street, irreverence for all forms of authority, a distrust of high-sounding words and attitudes, and a rich vein of linguistic humour such as is characteristic of border areas. While defenders of aesthetic values and literary purity, such as Rilke, looked on this phenomenon with distaste, Kafka throughout his life was attracted to the motley world of old Prague.

From the literary point of view, it is interesting to observe how the encounter of such varied pressures and picturesque contrasts led to the creation of new forms which, though irregular, untidy and grotesque, are nevertheless complex and full of meaning. The works of writers who have depicted this borderline world are generally elaborate in composition, significant at many levels, 'impure' linguistically and of inexhaustible meaning. This is true of Hasek's anti-hero and, in a very different way, of Kafka's work. At all events, qualities like these are much more important in Kafka than superficial references to the topography and history of Prague. We perceive here the complexity of his attitude towards his native city, and the national, religious and linguistic dilemma with which he was confronted from childhood until the end of his life.

Kafka's first day at school was September 16, 1889. Years later he described in a letter to Milena Jesenská the short walk from the house called Minuta on the Altstädter Ring to the German school on the Fleischmarkt: 'Our cook used to take me to school every morning. She was a thin, dried-up little woman with a pointed nose, hollow cheeks and a yellowish look, but firm, energetic and masterful. We lived in the house that separates the two squares; so we would walk across the Ring, then down the Teingasse, then through a kind of archway in the Fleischmarktgasse down to the Fleischmarkt. And every single morning for about a year, this is what would happen. Just as we left home, Cook would say that she was going to tell the teacher how naughty I had been. Most likely I hadn't in fact been so very naughty, only rather sullen and bad-tempered, melancholy and unhelpful—quite enough, of course, to make up a tale for the teacher's benefit. Knowing this, I did not take her threat lightly. But I thought, first of all, that it was miles and miles to school and that anything might happen on the way (of course, it wasn't really far at all—and that is how a child's apparent light-heartedness can gradually turn into anxiety and dead-eyed seriousness); and, secondly, at least while we were still crossing the Altstädter Ring, I doubted very much whether Cook, who was certainly a person in authority but only a domestic one, would really dare to open her mouth to the teacher, who was a person of authority in the great world. I might even say something of this kind, whereupon Cook usually answered curtly with her thin merciless lips that I could believe it or not as I pleased, but she was going to say it and that was that. Somewhere near the turning into the Fleischmarktgasse... the fear of Cook's threat got the better of me. School was frightening enough in itself, and here she was doing

Men and women crossing dark bridges,
past the statues of saints
with their faint glimmer of light.
Clouds drifting over grey skies,
past churches
with misty towers.
A man leaning over the parapet
and gazing into the river at evening,
his hands resting on ancient stone.

her best to make things worse. I began to plead, but she shook her head; the more I went on pleading, the more important the matter seemed and the more frightful the danger. I stood still and begged for forgiveness, she dragged me along; I threatened her with what my parents would do in retaliation, she laughed —here and now she was all-powerful; I held on to shop-doors and the cornerstones of buildings, refusing to go any further till she forgave me, I tugged at her skirt from behind—she had quite a time of it too, but she dragged me along saying it was one more thing to tell the teacher about; it was getting late, the clock on the Jakobskirche struck eight, the school bells were ringing, other children were starting to run; I was always terrified of being late, now we too had to run and I kept thinking "Will she tell or won't she?"—well, she never did tell, not a single time, but she always *might* have told, and it seemed as if she was more likely to each time—"I didn't tell yesterday but I will today, make no mistake about that"—and this was a weapon of which she never let go.'

The school was one for the less well-to-do boys, and most of them were from Prague Jewish families. Like the Gymnasium which Kafka attended later, it too was an arena of conflict. It was the first place where he came into real contact with the Prague milieu, and the street battles between Czech, German and Jewish youngsters—in which one of his future friends lost an eye—gave him an idea of national strife and other problems. The school does not seem to have effaced or altered the impressions made on him by the family circle. He remained a prisoner of the peculiar atmosphere in which his father 'governed the world from his armchair'. At all events the childhood impressions which he preserved in his highly accurate memory are confined to family events, and in general the family and its doings form the basis of his literary creativity.

'Perhaps you remember this too. One night I kept whimpering that I wanted a drink of water—not because I was thirsty, I'm sure of that, but probably just for fun, or to annoy you. You spoke sharply a few times and, as this had no effect, you hauled me out of bed on to the balcony and locked me out there for a while in my nightshirt. I don't say it was wrong of you, there may have been no other way to get a night's rest, but I recall it as typical of your way of bringing up a child and its effect on me. No doubt the incident made me obedient, but it inflicted a deep wound as well. My nature being what it was, I could never see a reasonable connection between asking for water without cause, which seemed a perfectly ordinary thing to do, and the terrifying experience of being stood out of doors. For

Pages 46/47 and 49: statues of saints on the Charles Bridge.

years afterwards I lived with the torturing thought that my father, with his supreme authority and his giant's strength, had, for almost no reason at all, come by night and dragged me out of bed on to the balcony, as though I meant absolutely nothing to him.'

One-sided as they may be, the childhood reminiscences contained in the Letter to his Father reflect an actual state of affairs. Hermann Kafka was a patriarch and an autocrat who brought up his children not by example, but by command and prohibition. In his eyes, his superior position gave him the right to condemn, threaten, mock and vituperate. This treatment had a crushing effect on the frail, sensitive boy and may well have been the cause of his desperate lack of confidence and paralyzing tendency to self-criticism in later years.

'As a child it was mostly at meal-times that I saw you, and so the things you taught me were mostly about how to behave at table. Every dish had to be emptied, everything on one's plate eaten up. The quality of the food must not be spoken of in any way—and yet you yourself often talked about it as "muck" and accused "that beast" (the cook) of spoiling it. You had a big appetite and liked to swallow down the food in large mouthfuls while it was still hot, so that I had to hurry to keep up with you; the gloomy silence was broken only by admonitions like "Eat before you talk" or "Come on, get a move on" or "There, you see, I've finished mine long ago." I wasn't allowed to crunch bones or slurp when I drank, but you were. It was of the highest importance to cut the bread straight, but there was no objection to your doing it with a knife dripping with gravy. I had to take care not to drop bits of food on to the floor, but there were more under your chair than anywhere. We were forbidden to do anything at table except eat—but you would cut and clean your nails, sharpen pencils or poke about in your ears with a toothpick. Please, Father, do not misunderstand me: these were trifles that would not have mattered in the slightest, the only reason they worried me was that you, the man whose authority and example mattered so enormously, did not keep the rules that you imposed on me. The result was that I thought of the world as divided into three parts. In the first one I lived, like a slave, subject to laws which were invented only for me and which, for some reason, I could never fully succeed in obeying. Then there was your world, infinitely far away, in which you played your part of governing and giving orders and being angry when they were not obeyed. And finally there was the third world, where everybody else lived, happy and free from all the business of obeying and commanding.'

The Vltava and the Charles Bridge. View of the Malá Strana from the Smetana Embankment.

With Ottla. Called for her at her English teacher's. Crossed over the embankment, stone bridges, a short distance through the Malá Strana, more bridges and so home. Inspiring statues of saints on the Charles Bridge. Wonderful summer evening light when the bridge is empty.

50

Franz's defence against his father's domineering consisted, besides attachment to his mother, in a kind of mimicry like that which a slave practises towards his owner.

'In order to hold my own just a little, and also in a sort of revenge, I soon began to watch out for small absurdities in you, to collect them and exaggerate them. For instance, the way in which you were dazzled by people of superior station, who generally were not superior in the least, and were always talking about what somebody with a Councillor's title had been saying or doing—and yet it hurt me at the same time that you, my father, should need to bolster your value and show off in such a way. Or your fondness for coming out with obscene words, in as loud a voice as possible, and then laughing as if you had said something witty instead of a mere petty indecency—of course this was just another sign of your vitality, and it put me to shame for that reason too. I noted all sorts of little foibles like this—they made me happy, and I used to whisper and joke about them. When you caught me at it you were angry and talked about spitefulness and disrespect—but believe me, it was only a means of self-preservation, and an ineffective one at that. My jokes were the kind that are told about gods and kings—not only compatible with the deepest reverence, but actually part of it.'

Kafka did well at his primary school and later at the Gymnasium—any statements to the contrary that he made later should be taken with a grain of salt. The Gymnasium was in the Kinsky Palace on the Altstädter Ring, a stately building erected by the famous Baroque architect Kilian Ignaz Dientzenhofer, who also built St. Nicholas's church not far off, next to the house where Kafka was born. Years later, the Kinsky Palace was also the site of Hermann Kafka's wholesale business, after he had risen in the world. No doubt he sent his son to the Gymnasium for practical reasons: it was a necessary prelude to the university, and this, in turn, was a natural lead-in to government service, which under the old monarchy offered early and substantial prospects.

The teaching method and syllabus conformed to the Central European pattern which, despite its conservatism, showed great vitality and maintained itself in Bohemia even after the fall of the monarchy. It was based on the classical languages (in some classes Kafka did ten hours of Greek and Latin out of a total of twenty-five hours a week), which were regarded as the surest foundation of literary culture and whose grammar served as the model for learning modern languages, including one's own. The teaching took the form of rigorous drilling in grammar

53

Graduating class at the Gymnasium, 1901.
Larger pictures in the centre: Kafka's teachers.
Top row, third from left: Franz Kafka.
Extreme left, second from bottom: Hugo Bergmann.
Bottom centre: Ewald Príbram.
Extreme right, second from bottom: Oskar Pollak.

Page 57: dedication of Franz Kafka in an album of Hugo Bergmann (1898).
Pages 54/55: the Tyn church silhouetted above the houses of the Old City.

rules and paradigms, and translation from the classical languages into German and vice versa. Of the spirit of ancient culture, the average schoolboy absorbed scarcely anything. The study of the mother-tongue and its literature was approached in a similarly unreal way, with arid anthologies based mainly on older works and reflecting a strong classical bias. More modern writings, and literary theory, were skimped; the theory of genres was not touched on at all. There was a great deal of memorizing and homework. Compulsory exercises included narrative and description, and in the higher forms essays and dissertations. Other subjects, apart from mathematics, did not figure largely in the curriculum. Czech, the second language of the country, was an optional subject like music, drawing or gymnastics.

The regime of the Altstädter Gymnasium was a strict one, and from the first class to the eighth there was a 'mortality' of fully seventy-five per cent. The pupils were made to use the back stairs, the main staircase being reserved for the masters, who in Bohemia, then as now, were called 'professors'. Some of Kafka's classmates were to become well known: Hugo Bergmann, a future professor of philosophy; Paul Kisch, who became editor of the *Neue Freie Presse* and was the brother of the 'fiery reporter' Egon Erwin Kisch; Oskar Pollak, a promising art historian who was killed in the First World War; and Emil Utitz,

a well-known professor of aesthetics. Their later memories of Kafka suggest that he was good at school but that there was a kind of veil between him and it: the Gymnasium evidently could not satisfy his inner needs and aspirations, either by developing his imagination or curing him of the anxiety and uncertainty born of family life. The result was that school became a link in the chain of causes that finally destroyed Kafka's relationship to the outside world.

It is not surprising, then, that no subject specially interested Kafka and that he looked outside school for stimulus in life. His schoolfellows relate that what little Jewish faith he had brought from home was extinguished by Spinozan pantheism, after which he and some of his friends were attracted by free thought. A deeper and more lasting intellectual interest was offered, towards the end of his school years, by Darwinism, under the influence of a master and of Oskar Pollak—his first real friend, a very mature boy for his years, who clearly influenced him deeply and with a certain authority. It was Pollak who introduced Kafka to the journal *Der Kunstwart*, which had a fundamental effect on his writing, causing him to adopt a style from which he did not break free for many years. Another fellow pupil who influenced him was Rudolf Illovy, who had socialist leanings and did not complete the Gymnasium course. Here as on later occasions, we repeatedly find Kafka striving to protect himself from the threat of isolation by associating with a wider group sharing common philosophical, political or religious views. The fact that he was never able to lose himself in them without reserve was due to his basic inability to embrace fundamental decisions of this kind, which belonged for him to the sphere of the impossible.

IV   THE UNIVERSITY YEARS

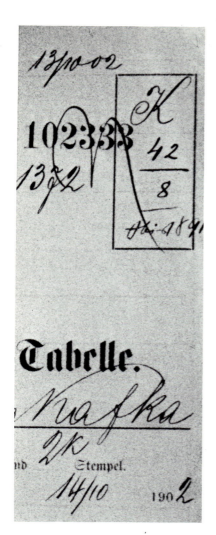

Passport record dated October 17, 1902: Kafka's acknowledgment of the receipt of a passport for the journey to Munich.

Kafka's entry into the university was accompanied by hesitation and doubt: this was chiefly the result of his father's influence, apart from the self-distrust which Franz had learned in the family circle and the years he had spent without distraction at school. His father's ideas of how best to make a living were in conflict with Franz's desire to pursue the humanities, literature and art, which had attracted him ever since, half-way through his schooldays, he began to write.

'When I embarked on some undertaking that you did not approve of, and you predicted that I would fail, my awe of your opinion was such that it became quite certain that I would fail, either then or at some later time. I lost all confidence in what I was doing.'

This presentation of his father as the cause of a trauma may in part be the result of a 'lawyer-like' exaggeration in later years; but there is no doubt that the elder Kafka's concern for his children's material future, and his 'feeling that something was going to waste, and must be forcibly rescued', took the form of insistent pressure which inevitably limited his son's freedom of action. Franz's natural reaction was to do his best to limit his dependence, financial and otherwise, on his parents and for that purpose to complete his studies in the shortest possible time, as in fact he did.

Before taking up law, however, which was the pursuit most likely to satisfy his father's practical ideas, he made one or two attempts to escape into other fields. Together with Oskar Pollak and Hugo Bergmann he first put himself down for chemistry, but after two weeks, unlike them, he dropped it and registered as a law student. He found the subject so distasteful and boring, especially on the historical side, that at the end of his first semester he transferred to German language and literature and the history of art.

Germanic studies in Prague were in the hands of August Sauer, a well-known commentator and enthusiast for the works of Grillparzer, Stifter and Hebbel. His general views were marked by a nationalist conception of the German cultural mission in Bohemia. He edited *Deutsche Arbeit*, a 'monthly devoted to German culture and the German spirit in Bohemia', which was founded in 1901 and was the central organ of the German community. Most of Kafka's teachers at the law faculty of the German university were contributors to it. Kafka was repelled by Sauer's type of nationalism and the spirit of German studies in Prague, and thought of pursuing the subject at Munich instead. He visited Munich in this connection: the date of his journey was long unknown, but documents recently found in

Præs. 13/10 02

Nro. Exh. 102333

Paß-Nr. 1372

K
42
8

Ai 1871

Paß-Tabelle.

Franz Kafka

Mit 1 Beilagen und 2K Stempel.

Paß ausgestellt am 14/10 190 2

Paß erhalten zu haben bestätigt:

Franz Kafka

Videat expedit

peto. Absendung der beil. Note an:

den Magistrat der königl. Hauptstadt Prag

die k. k. Bezirkshauptmannschaft in

sodann **ad acta.**

Prag, am 17/10 1902

Prague date it with fair accuracy. From the *Pass-Tabelle*, the police record of passports issued, it appears that on October 17, 1902 Kafka received one dated October 14 that was valid for a year; he had asked for permission to spend seventeen days abroad. His journey probably took place soon afterwards. As he was not yet of age under Austrian law, the document bears the indication 'Father's consent' with the signature 'Herman Kafka'. (Kafka senior spelt his first name variously at different times, with either one or two r's and one or two n's; 'Herman' is closest to the Czech form.) However, the plan to study in Munich fell through; Franz resumed the law course, and pursued it without further hesitation till he took his degree.

His idea of how to employ his life seems first to have taken shape at the university. The study of law—or, more precisely, 'legal and political sciences'—was merely a means of earning his daily bread. However, his attempt to combine personal interests with study, and later with the exercise of a profession, ended in disappointment. He accepted this with resignation and determined that he would never again try to merge his activity as a writer with his employment. The only advantage he saw in his career as a jurist was that it was 'indifferent' to him and had no effect on his inner life one way or the other.

'Consequently I was not really free to choose my profession. I knew that, compared with my main object, everything would be just as meaningless as it had been at school; so what I had to do was to find a profession, provided it were not too shaming to my vanity, that would leave me as indifferent as possible. The obvious one was law. This basic feeling on my part was only strengthened by small aberrations due to vanity or senseless hope, like a fortnight spent on chemistry or six months on German studies. So my choice fell on law, which meant that during the last few months before the exams, at great cost to my nerves, I lived exclusively on a kind of intellectual sawdust which thousands of others had already chewed over before me. In a certain way I actually liked it, as I liked the Gymnasium and afterwards my life as an official, since it fitted my situation perfectly well. At all events I showed great prescience, for even as a small child I foresaw well enough what study and a job were going to mean to me. I expected no salvation from them—I had long given up any such hope.'

This resigned attitude towards his profession was part of Kafka's 'flight into himself' and gradual shutting-out of the world. It meant, of course, that the possibility of finding an escape from solitude in his official career was from the start greatly diminished. As to finding an escape in other ways, such as marriage or especially his writing, the future was soon to show what the possibilities were.

From 1901 to 1906 Kafka was a student at the German University of Prague, the Karl-Ferdinand University. The state of affairs at the university, and the struggle in the latter part of the nineteenth century between its German and Czech elements, were a microcosm of the strife between nationalities and cultures in the city as a whole.

In 1882 two independent universities were set up, a Czech and a German one, both being regarded as legal successors of the Charles University. Thus in Kafka's time this dual system had existed for some time, and there were no legal or political disputes between the two universities. No one could be registered as a student or teacher at both, but this did not in practice prevent teachers from giving their services, or students from attending lectures, at the other university. The historic buildings of the Carolinum and Clementinum were used by both universities, but each was divided internally into a Czech and a German section with, as far as possible, their own entrances, stairs, corridors and lecture-rooms. The Carolinum, which Kafka usually attended for lectures on law, was especially segregated, with the entrance to the German university on the Eisengasse, and to the Czech one on the Obstmarkt. The famous Aula, in which degrees were (and still are) conferred, was used by either university on odd and even dates respectively; so were the archives and the library in the Clementinum, with which that of the Carolinum had been merged in Maria Theresa's time. In examinations the students of either university could choose whether they wished to be examined in German only or in German and Czech; Czech only was not permitted in Kafka's time, except for legal history.

The fact that the two nationalities coexisted so peacefully in a student community, in general so prone to excitement, confirms that around 1900 the worlds of Czech and German culture were largely uninterested in each other. The struggle over the university constitution had been long and troublesome, but once a policy decision had been taken which gave satisfaction to both sides, everyday life ran in separate channels which seldom merged.

From the lectures for which Kafka registered we may see what the basic course consisted of. The first semester was mainly legal history, and apart from a compulsory lecture on philosophy we find two on the history of art, reflecting his interest in this subject in the *Kunstwart* period. During his second semester, that devoted to German studies, he attended more

Interior of the Tyn church with window facing the apartment in which Kafka lived from 1896 to 1907.

View into the Tyn church from a
window of Kafka's apartment at
3 Zeltnergasse (Celetná).

lectures than at any other period: four on German literature (including two by Sauer), two on the German language, two on the history of art, one on music, one on psychology (by Anton Marty, a pupil of Franz Brentano), and one on classical philology. In later semesters he confined himself strictly to legal studies. Among his teachers were Professor Singer (canon law), Ulbrich (state law), the redoubtable Krasnopolski (civil law) and Rintelen (civics). The economist Alfred (brother of Max) Weber, who conferred Kafka's degree on him, was the most eminent member of the faculty, but Kafka did not attend his lectures. Most of those he did attend—for instance Professor Spiegel's—were dull and pedantic, and the course consisted chiefly of memorizing. He took his three final examinations, with somewhat better than average honours, between November 1905 and June 1906, and received his doctor's degree on June 18.

He found relief from his tedious studies in writing, which he had begun in earnest about three years before entering the university. Only a few fragments from that time have survived: in later years he ruthlessly burned what he called 'revolting old bits of paper'. His letters show that he was taking a close interest in literary affairs and was regularly reading several journals, notably *Der Kunstwart* (Munich), edited by Ferdinand Avenarius and described as a 'fortnightly review of poetry, drama, music, the plastic, graphic and applied arts'. This periodical, to which Kafka was introduced by his friend Oskar Pollak, was influenced by a Nietzschean cult of nature and creativity, and was mainly concerned with the fine arts in their broadest aspects. Its literary editors were Adolf Bartels, who extolled Hebbel as the 'greatest poet since Goethe', and Leopold Weber. The paper's style was original in a way that has gone rather flat; it rejected cosmopolitanism and modern art in the name of a 'pure' German style, whether of the past or present, with overtones of the movement known as *Heimatkunst*. Its quest for originality and healthy primitivism was not devoid of affectation. For some years Kafka was attracted by its bizarre, artificial and precious tone, as appears from the style and vocabulary of his letters at that time. This is the only instance of his adhering without reserve to a model presented from outside; at all other times, his life and writings are marked by a refusal to adapt or compromise.

Kafka's attachment to the *Kunstwart* helped to liberate him from the influence of Prague German literature, the writers of which were like an ever-shrinking island surrounded by a rising tide. When Kafka came in contact with them their work

Right, and pages 70/71: St. Vitus's Cathedral in the Hradcany Castle.

So K. began to move off slowly, tiptoeing along the pew as far as the broad nave, up which he walked undisturbed; however, the flagstones echoed to the quietest footfall and the vaulting repeated the sound, faintly but continuously, in a regular, manifold progression. K. felt forlorn and isolated as he advanced between the rows of empty pews, with the priest's eyes fixed on him for all he knew, and the size of the cathedral seemed to him to border on the extreme limit of what a human being could bear.

and its problems were conditioned by the fact that they were cut off from vital sources. This was true not only in the social and psychological sphere but above all in that of language, the essential basis of literature. The German written and spoken in Prague at that time was a stiff, petrified idiom, the dialect basically of a single class. It was a long time since it had been refreshed by the living language of town or countryside; the social movement had failed to enrich it, slang had passed it by. It was dead and prosaic, austerely official and sparse in vocabulary. Slowly but surely, however, it was undergoing the vivifying influence of Czech, both in intonation and in phraseology and syntax.

In Kafka's youth, most of the Prague writers in German were obsessed by this situation and by the impoverishment of their literary and spoken tongue. They endeavoured to overcome its poverty, as is usual in such cases, by a forced originality, an artificial and literary search for uncommon words. Their obsession with the language was compounded by social and psychological factors, by loss of contact with the real world, lack of interest in contemporary problems, and fear of their own decline. The upshot was a curiously unreal literature: artificial and over-refined, psychological and laboriously erotic, romanticized and hankering after the past; linguistically hybrid, full of rhetoric and unpruned fantasy, 'literary' in a café or drawing-room style, and showing off in a self-conscious attempt to conceal its own poverty. For such writers as Meyrink, Leppin, and also the young Franz Werfel, Rilke and Brod, literature was a safety-valve for deep feelings that went to the roots of their very existence in Prague. It may be that this explains the literary quality of the whole of Prague German culture at the time, when writing books appears to be first and foremost a social phenomenon.

Kafka, for his part, was from the outset opposed to the Prague literary school, most of whose work he rejected or viewed with indifference. As time went on he worked out for himself a new relationship with the language at his and their disposal. Accepting it with all its stiffness, scanty vocabulary and official severity (a 'language fit for public notices'), he succeeded by dint of deep understanding, from the inside as it were, in turning it into a proper instrument for his purposes. Whereas, for example, Prague German literature is characterized by strings of would-be striking adjectives and similes, Kafka confines himself to a plain description without comment. Whereas the other writers pile up images in an attempt to outdo the reader's fancy, Kafka gives him no more than what is needed for his fancy to do its own service. The same applies, *mutatis mutandis*, to the choice and elaboration of themes, where literature of the Prague school startles us by its eccentricity and extravagance. Literature was one of the fields in which, for many years, Kafka sought to link himself with the outside world, but as time went on he became more and more out of sympathy with the German writers of his native city. In the end his contact with them was reduced to a very small, unsystematic range of authors —some alive, but more of them dead—and works which in one way or another had struck through to his inner world.

One of the many 'impossibilities' from which Kafka suffered was that of penetrating his Czech surroundings. His own feeling about the Czech element in Prague and its hinterland was that it was an irresistible force, full of biological and cultural vitality, asserting its rights without fear of denial and justly confident of the future. He differed in this from his German contemporaries, who either ignored their Czech fellow citizens or looked on them and their history with a detached form of romantic idealism, as a picturesque piece of national folklore or as a childlike people with the charm of youth, engaged in learning the business of life and developing a culture of their own. Kafka perceived the superiority of the Czechs as a young, healthy element whose strength was not sapped by historical scepticism, and in addition he felt towards them a sense of inescapable guilt.

Unlike most German writers in Prague he had a good knowledge of Czech, which he read and wrote fluently—his Czech writings contain no more 'mistakes' than those of the best Czech authors—and with a feeling for the nuances of colloquial speech. He went to see Czech performances at the National Theatre and frequented city taverns with their hybrid atmosphere which seems to have especially appealed to him. Although the Czechs themselves later somewhat exaggerated the strength of his links with them, thus testifying to their interest in a great fellow townsman and to a certain trait of the Czech character, Kafka's interest in his Czech surroundings was more than superficial, as many of his thoughts and observations make clear. Despite his inability to identify with Czech national feeling, he took a steady interest in contemporary Czech literature and was well acquainted with it. It is noteworthy that he treats it with sympathy even when pointing out its faults, which as an acute critic he was bound to do.

In the last quarter of the nineteenth century Czech literature was dominated by two schools, which were in many ways

opposed to each other. The national school, led by Svato-
pluk Cech, invoked the basic ideas of the Czech national
awakening, including history progressivism and Slav solidarity;
it did so in a romantic and rather conservative fashion, which
corresponded well enough to the patriotic feelings of the dominant elements in Czech society. The opposite school, represented by the *Lumír* generation, was cosmopolitan in tendency,
regarding it as the chief need of the time to 'open windows
on to Europe' and thus to promote Czech national emancipation by modern means. The authors of this school, headed
by Jaroslav Vrchlicky, translated in quite a short time an extraordinary amount of foreign literature, both old and new,
introduced various foreign poetical forms and largely succeeded
in transforming the spirit of Czech poetry.

Then came the nineties and the *fin de siècle*, marked in the Czech
lands by a literary revolution: an impetuous assault by the
young generation of poets and critics led by F. X. Salda, with
bold, new ideas which, though chaotic at first, represented a
ruthless attempt to re-evaluate all values. Taine and his fol-
lowers, Nietzsche, Ruskin and the English aesthetic movement
—every contemporary impulse was used to buttress the new
assessment of the nation's history and problems, the meaning
of its culture and the orientation of its literature. Vrchlicky
was written off as the erector of a pyramid of paper. The new
century opened with feverish activity in all directions, new
ideas and trends for which the Czech lands provided a fertile
soil and a lively welcome.

The one voice missing in the chorus was that of German literature, in Prague and elsewhere in the country. Wherever the
two cultures encountered each other there was a lack of interest, which today seems incomprehensible. German journals in
Prague publish embarrassed excuses when their readers ask why
they do not carry reports on Czech cultural life. In much the
same way, Czech periodicals have no room for reports on the
German literature of Prague, whose problems should be of
such interest to the country. Czechs at that time were deliberately concentrating their attention on French culture, as a
counterweight to the German influence, which had so deeply
affected their country's past. This was a long-term orientation
and went far to determine the development of Czech culture.
Kafka's connection with the Czech literary world was a rather
slight one; we owe it in part to his friendship with Milena
Jesenská and in part to the left-wing poet and editor S. K. Neumann, who 'discovered' Kafka more promptly than most
Czech critics.

A tower and alleyway in the Prague
quarter 'Zu den Mühlen'.

*Not only Prague, but the whole world
is tragic. All protective walls are
smashed by the iron fist of technology.
This is not expressionism, but naked
everyday life. We are brought face to
face with reality as a criminal is
brought to the block.*

As a student Kafka sought contacts in contemporary Prague in accordance with his cultural interests and his urge to escape from inner uncertainty. He attended lectures and literary evenings, which he criticized in his letters and Diary with his usual terseness and penetration. As a result, no doubt, of his experience at school, he did not join clubs and associations, though Prague in his day was full of invitation to do so. There were several German or German-Jewish students' associations, which vied with one another in professional rivalry and in conflicts on political issues. Kafka seems most often to have visited the assimilationist *Rede- und Lesehalle deutscher Studenten* (German —later 'Jewish'—students' debating society and library) in the Ferdinandstrasse, which had a considerable library and public reading room and organized literary talks and writers' evenings, including addresses by German and Austrian authors; it was also intended to be an 'association and representative body of Jewish-national university students of both sexes'. This was where Kafka first met Max Brod in 1902, about two years before they actually became friends: on that occasion Brod had given a talk in which he spoke slightingly of Nietzsche, whom Kafka admired under the influence of *Der Kunstwart*.

That influence in fact dates from the end of Kafka's schooldays. During his student period, as Klaus Wagenbach has discovered, he became, perhaps through his teacher Anton Marty, a member of the 'Brentanists', who used to meet in the Louvre café, also in the Ferdinandstrasse; but it is not clear how strongly he was influenced by the circle and its philosophy. Later its debates were transferred in part to the home of the chemist Fanta, a meeting-place of the German intellectual élite, including at various times Albert Einstein, the physicist Philipp Frank, the mathematician Gerhard Kowalewski, and Kafka's friends Hugo Bergmann, Felix Weltsch and Max Brod. The salon was dominated by the lady of the house, a gentle, idealistic soul, who began by being interested in Nietzsche and Indian philosophy and later took up Rudolf Steiner's theosophy, to which she no doubt introduced Kafka.

All these contacts have one feature in common which is typical of the young Kafka: his participation in public and private cultural activities and debates, and his relationship to people outside his own immediate circle, were timid and more or less indirect. Those who were present on such occasions described him as an interested, but detached and usually silent spectator. However, he followed the proceedings with absolute seriousness, as is often apparent from some lapidary comment. The barrier of shyness was one that he found it hard to overcome

Franz Kafka shortly before receiving his doctorate of law.

The writer Max Brod.

Max Brod on Kafka: 'An extraordinary strength emanated from him, the like of which I have not found even in encounters with very important and famous men.'

all his life. He was brought into contact with people and institutions by his friends, especially Max Brod, whom we have also to thank for the fact that Kafka actually published his work: left to himself, he would have thought it sufficient to write it. As time went on, Kafka found it harder and harder to make contact with the world, till finally all the roads were barred.

Dr. František R. Kraus

V PROFESSION AND VOCATION

On leaving the university Kafka was confronted with the choice of a career. The decision was not a particular urgent one, but it was natural to choose one of the professions to which a law degree opened the way. Towards the end of his studies he had already worked as a lawyer's clerk in the office of his uncle Richard Löwy on the Altstädter Ring. After leaving the university he was obliged to gain a year's legal experience before he could enter Government service. This he did, curiously enough, in the provincial court and later the criminal court in Prague, although he never contemplated becoming either a lawyer or a judge.

Various ideas about his future occupation arose and were discarded during the year in question. 'Other people take a decision once in a while and rest pleasantly on it in between; but I keep taking decisions incessantly, as often as a boxer—the only

Covering letter of the Prague office to Kafka's application

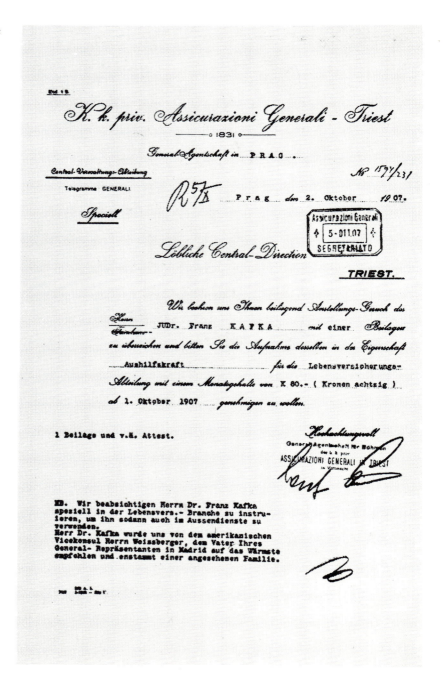

thing is, I don't act on them.' For a time he longed to live abroad, as an escape from an office in Prague, and there was some practical possibility of this, as two of his mother's brothers had substantial jobs in foreign countries. Alfred Löwy, who was general manager of the Spanish railways in Madrid, visited Prague often and seems to have had quite an effect on Kafka's thoughts about his career. Towards the end of his year of court work Kafka wrote to Brod:

'No, if my prospects haven't improved by October I shall take the course at the Commercial Academy and do Spanish in addition to French and English. It would be nice if you came too: my impatience would make up whatever lead you have over me. My uncle could get us jobs in Spain or, if not, we could go to South America, the Azores or Madeira.'

Uncle Alfred did not produce a job in Spain, but he used his influence with the Trieste insurance company Assicurazioni Generali, which had a branch on Wenceslas Square in Prague. Recommended by the Madrid representative of the company, Kafka took up the Prague job on October 1, 1907. 'Here I am in the office. The firm is the Assicurazioni Generali, and there seems a reasonable chance that one day I shall sit in an armchair in some far-away country and look out through the window at sugar-cane fields or Moslem cemeteries—insurance interests me anyway, but the work I am doing at the moment is dreary.'

The building of the 'Assicurazioni Generali' on Wenceslas Square: post-card from Kafka to his friend Max Brod.

The Workers' Insurance Office (at Naporící 7, Prague), in which Kafka worked until he retired owing to illness in 1922.

Page 83: a corridor on the fourth floor of the Insurance Office.

Kafka's dreams did not last long. The company with its world-wide branches did not offer him any inspiring work, and the terms of service were hard. In his application he had undertaken if necessary to work overtime 'without entitlement to special pay'; in return he was given the right to a fortnight's leave every other year. Apart from office managers and heads of departments, employees were not allowed 'to keep, in the desks and cupboards assigned to them, any other papers or objects than those of the company, and these should be locked up.' On the application form Kafka stated that he knew Czech in addition to French and English, but was out of practice in these two languages. In reply to a question about his financial state he wrote: 'My parents support me.' When he was taken on, the branch office wrote to Trieste: 'We propose to train Dr. Franz Kafka especially in life insurance, with a view to later employing him abroad.' His starting salary as a temporary assistant was 80 kronen a month. The worst feature from his point of view was that the working hours were from 8 a.m. to 6 p.m.

'My life is in a very untidy state. I have a job with the minute salary of 80 kronen and an interminable working day of eight to nine hours. As for the rest of the time, I gobble it up like a wild beast. I have never before had to cram my daily life into six hours, and what with learning Italian and wanting to spend these pleasant evenings out of doors, my free time leaves me in a rather exhausted state.'

As soon as his job began Kafka was involved in a fundamental conflict between his public and private life, the office and literature. This conflict was never resolved; some years later he wrote of it as 'a frightful double life which can probably end only in madness.' The combination of two incompatible tasks, on each of which he was dependent in a different way, affected his whole life and made his situation an inextricable one.

While still working at the Assicurazioni Generali he wrote to his friend Hedwig W., whom he had met when staying with his uncle Siegfried at Triesch ('Trest' in southern Moravia): 'I have had a frightful week, far too much to do at the office, perhaps it will be like this always—oh well, one has to earn the right to one's grave.' Or again: 'But it is not only laziness [i. e. his failing to write]—it is fear as well, fear of the business of writing—a terrible occupation, yet how miserable I am now at being deprived of it!'

He hankered after a more convenient working day such as the regular 8 a.m. to 2 p.m. customary in public offices and a few private ones. His dream was no longer to see foreign lands but

to have time in which to write. Soon after taking up his first job he began to cast about for another: for a time he had in mind the post office. In the middle of 1908 he began looking around in earnest, and with the help of his schoolmate Ewald Príbram, who in the past had introduced him to Prague society, he was appointed on July 30 to a post in the Workers' Insurance Office for Bohemia in the Porschitscherstrasse: Príbram's father was then its chairman of directors. Here the hours were much more convenient, and the working day ended at 2 p.m. Business was conducted in German and Czech, and Kafka's application was drawn up in both languages. Documents that have survived in the office give a good idea of his work. Within a year he was promoted to the rank of probationer, and his superiors expressed a high opinion of him. Under the heading 'Energy and interest in work' they wrote: 'Extremely industrious; takes a keen interest', and also 'Combines great industry with a steady interest in all aspects of the work. Has also given much of his free time to office matters.' Under 'Quality of work' we read 'Excellent', and under 'General remarks': 'Dr. Kafka is an extremely hard worker of outstanding ability and with a keen sense of duty.'

His work was spoken of in this vein throughout his official career until the onset of his illness, with emphasis on his ambition, conscientiousness and good manners towards his colleagues and superiors. His duties consisted mainly of preventing injury to workers, classifying industrial establishments and factories according to the degree of danger involved, and considering the appeals of management against decisions in this respect. His work entailed frequent trips to the countryside, especially to the German industrial areas of northern Bohemia. At the outset he worked for a short time in the technical department, then for some months in the accident department, then back to the technical. His zeal was soon shown in reports of some length, which were printed in the office journal and elsewhere. One of these related to compulsory insurance in the building trade, another to motor insurance (a novelty at the time); other titles were 'Accident prevention measures' and 'Accident insurance and the employer'. All these questions raised numerous problems and involved disputes with managers, who often refused to insure their workers or contested the allocation of their works to this or that safety category.

Kafka rose from the rank of a probationer (1909) to that of a clerk (1910), junior secretary (1913), secretary (1920) and senior secretary (1922). From time to time he addressed requests to his superiors regarding his promotion and pay, and

How humble these people are—they come to us with requests! Instead of storming into the office and smashing it to bits, they come with requests.

Gustav Janouch's father, an office colleague of Kafka's.

these were generally granted in whole or in part. In one extensive submission of this kind he pleaded the cause of the junior clerks in general and showed with full statistics how unfairly they had been treated, by comparison with other employees, in previous salary adjustments. On his own behalf he regularly invoked the rising cost of living and also his academic background and age. Another group of documents are his applications for vacation or, after the onset of his illness, for the grant or extension of vacation on health grounds, and letters explaining his absence from the office on account of ill-health or indisposition.

When Kafka joined the Insurance Office it was going through a crisis and showing a large annual deficit. For a short time past it had had a new chief, Robert Marschner, a lecturer in insurance at the German technical university of Prague; he took a liking to Kafka, as did Eugen Pfohl, the head of his department. Kafka already knew them both, having heard them lecture, when he was still with the Assicurazioni Generali, in a course on workers' insurance at the Commercial Academy. Under Marschner the affairs of the Office soon looked up, thus improving Kafka's prospects also. In later years he was on equally good terms with its Czech director, Bedrich Ostrcil, who was a lecturer on social insurance and also the brother of a well-known Czech composer.

The office premises were large and imposing. As Gustav Janouch writes, 'The whole building was so massive and dignified that the poor invalids and work-people who were summoned to draw their pension or receive compensation for injury usually looked bewildered and intimidated from the moment they glimpsed the porter with his enormous beard.'

The documents drawn up by Kafka are distinguished by brilliant logic, an acute legal sense and elegance of style. There is a complete absence of rhetorical adornment and verbiage, nor do they fall into bureaucratic cliché. The style is directly subservient to the matter in hand, just as it is in the very different context of his literary work.

After 1918 he corresponded with the Office in Czech. These letters, together with the few others that he wrote in Czech, and some documents from police archives, prove that he had a good command of the language. Such 'mistakes' as occur are of the kind that Czech writers themselves frequently make. They concern such matters as the inflections of pronouns or indications of the length of vowels: the latter reflect colloquial usage and show that Kafka had learned Czech primarily as a spoken language.

The letters to the Office during his last years are essentially a record of the development of his mortal illness. They show his anxious sense of duty and awareness of the difficulty his absence was causing: his requests for extensions of leave are made with diffidence, and always with an exact time-limit.

The division of his time between office work and literature grew more irksome as time went on: it constantly threatened the delicate balance of his existence and the closed circle within which his life was led. For years he sought a permanent way of escape, till in the end it appeared that only the search was permanent:

'My happiness, my talent and any power I have to be of use— all these have long been bound up with literature... But there are many reasons why I cannot give myself up completely to literature as I should. Even apart from the question of my family, I could not make a living as a writer because of the peculiar character of my works and the slowness with which I produce them; nor have I the health or the temperament to embrace a life which at the very best is bound to be uncertain. So I became an insurance official instead. But the two ways of life are impossible to reconcile, and there is no way of being happy in both at once. The least success in one means a great unsuccess in the other. If I write something good one evening, next day in the office I am wild with excitement and can't work properly. The tussle gets worse and worse. I do my duty outwardly in the office, but not inwardly, and this is a source of unhappiness that I cannot throw off.'

Between September 1917, when his illness broke out, and the end of June 1922, when he was pensioned, Kafka spent long months on sick and convalescent leave. In a letter of June 7, 1922, asking to be placed on the retired list, he wrote: 'My health has improved substantially since I was allowed to undergo systematic treatment, but in my doctor's view it is not yet such that I could undertake regular work without the risk of my lung condition deteriorating so that I should soon have to ask for another period of leave. As I do not wish to make such a request and as the doctor assures me that, given proper care and rest for the next four months or so, my health will be sufficiently improved for me to return to work without fear of another interruption, I hereby respectfully ask that I may be placed in temporary retirement, with the enjoyment of my pension rights for as long as this retirement may last.'

The idea of retirement had already been put forward in October 1921 in a certificate by Dr. Kodym, which concluded with the words: 'The final outcome cannot be predicted, but

The peace among the old houses has the effect of a charge of explosive destroying all internal barriers. As your feet run down the hill your voice creates, word by word, a mountain of imagery. The frontier between the outside and the inside world disappears. You plunge through the streets as though through dark sewers of time. You listen to your own voice and it sounds exceptionally clever and witty, but what you hear is only a convulsive attempt at concealing your own self-depreciation. You look, as it were, contemptuously over your shoulder at yourself. It would not take much for you to fish out a pen and scribbling-block and write yourself an anonymous letter.

Postcard from Ouvaly with a drawing by Kafka.

Ottla's little morning snack

Herrn I. U. C. Josef David, Prague IV
16. 5. 1915
I have come a long way already, and here I am sitting in an inn and looking forward to what comes next. Much love meanwhile. It is only 11 a. m.
Ottla
Cordial greetings F. Kafka
Best wishes Irma Stein

a complete cure is unlikely. It is for consideration, therefore, whether retirement on pension would not be the best course from the patient's point of view and also from that of the Insurance Office.'

At the end of 1923 Kafka sought permission from his director to move to Steglitz near Berlin but to have his pension remitted through his parents, as he would suffer financially if it were sent otherwise. 'Steglitz is a semi-rural suburb of Berlin, a kind of garden city. I live in a small villa with a garden of its own and it is half an hour's walk to the forest. There are big botanical gardens ten minutes away, and my home is surrounded by gardens in every direction.' Permission was duly received; Kafka's acknowledgment runs: 'With reference to your letter No. 1152/23 of December 31, for which I respectfully thank you, I hereby authorize my parents, Hermann and Julie Kafka, resident at Prague, Staroměstské náměstí 6, 3rd floor, to receive the pension instalments due to me. I will forward regularly my life certificate, duly attested.'

The last sentence is not a dream or a fantastic error: the ways of bureaucracy required that Kafka, pensioned off and stricken by a mortal illness, should at regular intervals certify to his employers that he was still alive. A human being must 'earn the right to his grave', but even when imminent death interrupts his work he must, in the interests of good order, furnish evidence of his continued existence... This is not the only 'Kafkaesque' incident in the correspondence: there is a real though mysterious link between the creative artist's own life and that of his characters and inventions.

In early years he sought refuge from loneliness and from the oppression of his job in travelling with friends in and about Prague, in the countryside or abroad. His relationship to the world was probably never more free and open than immediately after he left the university. At that time he went in for sport, artistic entertainment and the society of his fellows, and would spend whole nights in the cabarets of Prague, often in the company of girls of easy virtue. This life had all the marks of a transitional existence: the longing to write was suppressed, and the vital problems of anxiety and insecurity were held at bay by superficial diversions. Whatever he wrote at this period was stylized, playful and decorative. His excursions to the country were not undertaken for the country's sake but in order to escape from himself and from office work. We can learn from Max Brod what a far-off place the country was to those city intellectuals, who could be startled out of their wits by the chirping of a cricket: 'Two friends and I spent the holiday weekend in the country. We got as far as Dobrschichovice on the Beraun river... We were startled by a sharp, shrill noise that seemed to come from the green and white villas, blazing with light... Apparently they were crickets. How were we townspeople to know that?'

Kafka's trips to the country or abroad were an escape from the turmoil of Prague and the family circle, from insecurity and the constraint of everyday life; they lent him a new vision, a fresh outlook, a livelier sense of humour. During these years, mostly on Max Brod's suggestion and in his company, Kafka visited the Italian lakes, Paris (twice) and Weimar. His friendship with Brod was at its height at this time: it was renewed after a break in 1914, but he does not seem to have reposed so much confidence in it then as in his youth. Later, if he undertook such journeys it was usually by himself: they were mostly connected with marriage plans or with his health, and they became less frequent until the time when he lost contact with the world altogether.

For a short period he sought a refuge in theosophy, to which he was evidently introduced by the Fanta family: at this time

Rudolf Steiner himself was giving lectures in Prague, to the keen interest of the Imperial and Royal police. Kafka's attempt to make closer contact with Steiner and his teaching ended in a comic misunderstanding, by which his interest in the subject was rapidly cured.

Another arduous quest was the rediscovery of Judaism, which for years had seemed to Kafka an outworn and empty form. His interest was first seriously reawakened by the arrival in 1911–12 of a travelling company of Galician actors. Kafka attended their performances (in Yiddish) at the Savoy café in the Old City and wrote dozens of pages about them in his Diary; he praised their talents and became a friend of a member of the troupe named Isaak Löwy. The insight he obtained into their peculiar world made him aware of links between himself and Jewry that he had not suspected, and removed the first veils of misunderstanding. In the course of time he explored further, but without ever pursuing the subject to its end.

From 1909 and especially from 1912 onwards, the external world became less important to Kafka as a refuge from his inner troubles. He became more and more involved in the narrow sphere of family life, his immediate friends, office work by day, writing in the evenings, abortive marriage plans and illness. Such is the background of all Kafka's writing—the struggle for peace against the din of the outside world, for balance against his own instability and that of his surroundings, for strength against impotence, for permanence against destruction, for sanity against the absurd and for truth against the lies of this world. Although his experience of life was reduced to the narrowest possible confines, it was expressed in words of unparalleled intensity for his day.

'I must go and see my sister and her baby. The night before last, when my mother came home at one in the morning with the news that my sister had had a baby boy, my father roamed through the apartment in his nightshirt, flung doors open, woke up the servants and my sisters and me and announced the event as though the child had not only been born, but had led a distinguished life and was already being buried.'

Jottings from private life, with no special attempt at style, turn into literature under Kafka's pen—an unusual phenomenon in German Prague, with its emphasis on literary form. Kafka, for instance, publishes the following entry from his Diary without in any way altering the details that relate it to his own family: 'I sit down to write, though my brow is constantly quivering and my room is a noise-centre for the whole apartment. I hear every door bang, the only sound it drowns for me is that of

Pages 92/93: the Jewish cemetery in the Old City of Prague.

the people rushing across the rooms; I even hear the oven being slammed shut in the kitchen. My father flings open the door of my room and strides across it in his trailing nightshirt; the ashes are being raked out of the stove next door; Valli, standing in the hall, screams like someone in a Paris street to ask if Father's hat has been brushed; a voice answers in a hissing tone, supposedly for my benefit. The front door is unlatched with a bronchial rattle, then opens wider, singing for a moment with a woman's voice, then shuts again with a dull masculine thud, which is the harshest sound to the ear... Now that Father has gone out there is a softer, vaguer, more hopeless noise, with the two canaries' voices predominating. Hearing them, I wonder once again if I should not open the door a tiny bit, creep into the next room like a snake and, lying there on the ground, beg my sisters and their governess to be quiet.'

The Jewish people are scattered about the world like seed. As a grain of corn absorbs food from its environment and stores it up to foster its own growth, so it is the destiny of Jewry to absorb the forces of humanity into itself, to purify them and lead them to a higher plane. Moses is still alive today. As Dathan and Abiram resisted him with the words 'Lo naale: we will not come up', so the world resists us with the cry of anti-Semitism. Rather than rise to what is human, mankind plunges into the depths of the zoological theory of race. Beating up Jews, they murder human beings.

K

612

is

t

i pas.

VI NEW DOCUMENTS

Kafka's office work, and contacts with offices in general, played a large part in his life. By his legal calling he was associated with the Imperial and Royal bureaucracy which was, in its time, one of the most perfect in the world, and which enjoyed the whole-hearted respect of the German-Jewish enclave in Prague, to which Kafka belonged. The state and municipal administration, the courts, banks and social insurance offices were a self-contained world which the individual citizen approached with proper deference. Its impeccable routine, while over-ceremonious for present-day taste, was stamped with an impersonal dignity which at all points stood opposed to mere private convenience. The peace of mind and civic respectability of the inhabitants of Prague depended on the prompt and conscientious fulfilment of their obligations towards the bureaucratic machine. A rigid, precise, impersonal style was prescribed for contacts with it; human raw material was accepted and processed in accordance with exact regulations. This unceasing activity and unremitting vigilance was to some a source of security, while others felt insecure and threatened by the mighty, enigmatic force with its elaborate powers of scrutiny and record.

One of the main themes of Kafka's stories is this confrontation between the citizen and the authorities—between the private individual and the remorseless machine which subjects him to a never-ending process of law. The author expresses in many different ways his conception of human fate in the clutches of bureaucracy. It may not be out of place, therefore, for us to look at Kafka through the eyes of officialdom, by examining the documents concerning him in police files and those of the military and civil administration.

Investigations in Prague recently brought to light relevant documents from the civil and police archives, and it has been possible to follow up references to Kafka in the latter. This is a matter of especial interest since all his biographers lay stress on his relations, before the First World War, with the numerous anarchistic and anti-militaristic groups in Prague, which were the object of police surveillance and persecution. Their statements are all based on a common source, namely the revelations made by the former Czech anarchist Michal Mares as late as 1946.

Prominence is usually given to Kafka's relations with the Young People's Club, which was a centre of the anarchist youth of Prague. It had been founded in Královské Vinohrady in 1900 under the name of the Young Generation Club, as a harmless educational society: Article 21 of its statutes declared that 'The

Document on pp. 99 and 100: application from Dr. Franz Kafka, resident at 3 Zeltnergasse, Prague, for a certificate of good behaviour for the purpose of entering Government service.

An die hochlöbliche

k. k. Polizeidirektion

in Prag.

Dr. Franz Kafka, wohnhaft in Prag, Zeltnergasse N3 bittet um Ausstellung eines Heimatscheines zum Zwecke der Ausführung einer Auslandsreise

Dr. Franz Kafka

Eltern: Hermann Kafka, Kaufmann,
Julie geb Löwi

Geschwister: Gabriele, Valerie, Ottilie —

Geburtsdatum: 1883, Religion mosaisch,
wohlverhalten.

An die löbliche

k. k. Polizeidirektion

in Prag!

2 K. Stempel

geb!
19/9 906

Dr. Franz Richter, wohnhaft
in Prag, Zeltnergasse N 3 bittet
um Abstellung eines Verbesse-
rungsgesuches.

Club shall not be associated with any political activity.' Its members at that time were mainly Czech Socialists, but before long the anarchists gained control: in 1903 it changed its name and adopted a new statute according to which its purpose was 'to enter into contact with other non-political associations pursuing similar aims, and to form a union with them'. From then until 1910 it organized lectures on hotel premises in various parts of Prague. These were regularly attended by police officers, and from their detailed reports we can learn many interesting facts about the lectures and discussions, the number of those present (it varied from 20 to 250) and sometimes their names. Among those who gave lectures was the Czech politician Václav Klofáč, in 1901, on the cultural and social influence of Karel Havlícek Borovsky, the nineteenth-century patriotic writer and politician—this was one of two meetings in the club's history that were dispersed by the police. The Czech poet S. K. Neumann, then a leading anarchist, lectured on the French journalist and anarchist Zo d'Ax (1902); the anarchist Vohryzek on Max Stirner (1902) and on socialism (1907); Michal Kácha, an anarchist and an acquaintance of Kafka's, on Kropotkin (1905) and anarchist morality (1908); the philosopher and sociologist Emanuel Chalupny on Christian socialism (1904); and Jaroslav Hasek, the creator of the Good Soldier Schweik, on political economy (1907). In 1905 the club transferred its headquarters to the Karolinenthal district, and the police grew increasingly suspicious of its activity. In 1906 they forbade it to make a collection for the wives and children of unemployed miners in north Bohemia (a stronghold of anarchists), and the official report describes it at this time as 'a society most of whose members belong to the National Socialist party, and which sets out to make young people acquainted with anarchist theories.' About 1907 the young Czech socialists were carrying on a good deal of anti-militarist activity, inciting recruits to disobey orders and refuse to take the oath of loyalty. An anti-militarist congress was actually convened in Prague; it was broken up by the police, the organizers were put on trial and several clubs dissolved. The Young People's Club was spared for the time being, but it became increasingly radical under the leadership of the cultivated Vlastimil Borek; stormy meetings were held in Dufek's Inn on Zizka street in Karolinenthal, and the club was closely watched by the police under the noted persecutor of anarchists, Inspector Karel Slavícek. A meeting held in April 1910 on the subject of Militarism and Patriotism was the main pretext for its dissolution in October of that year, which was also reported in the German Prague

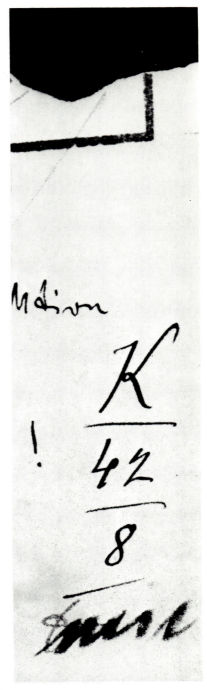

Document on pp. 102–5: supplementary request dated September 25, 1916, in which Kafka asks that his application for permission to cross the frontier in order to travel to Munich should 'not be dealt with for the time being.'

An die hohe

k.k.Statthalterei
/ Departement VIII /

P r a g .

JUDr. F r a n z K a f k a , Vicesekre-
tär der Arbeiter-Unfall-Versicherungs-
Anstalt für das Königreich Böhmen in
Prag legt zu seinem Gesuch vom 15.1.
betreffend die Bewilligung der Grenzüberschreitung für eine Reise nach
München ein Nachtragsgesuch vor .

1 Beilage

Hohe

k.k.Statthalterei !

        Der ergebenst Gefertigte , Dr.F r a n z   K a f k a
Vicesecretär der Arbeiter-Unfall-Versicherungs-Anstalt für das
Königreich Böhmen in Prag hat unter dem 16.1.M. beim k.k.Polizei-
Präsidium ein Gesuch um Bewilligung der Grenzüberschreitung nach
München eingebracht . In diesem Gesuch war entsprechend dem damals
beiliegenden Brief der Galerie Hans Goltz die Grenzüberschreitung
für den Monat Oktober erbeten . Nun soll aber nach dem beiliegenden
Schreiben vom 22.1.M. die Vorlesung , zu welcher die Grenzüber-
schreitung angesucht wurde, erst im November stattfinden. Das genau
Datum wird erst in cca. 10 Tagen bekannt gegeben werden können.
        Der regebenst Gefertigte ändert also in dieser
Hinsicht sein ursprüngliches Gesuch, welches nach Mitteilung des
zuständigen Departemente der k.k.Polizei-Direktion bereits an die
k.k.Statthalterei abgegangen ist und bittet die k.k.Statthalterei,
das Gesuch solange vorläufig unerledigt zu lassen, bis der ergebens
Gefertigte das geraue Datum angeben kann.

        P r a g , am 25.September 1916.

                              Dr Franz Kafka
                              Prag Porič 7

Datum wird erst in ced. 14 Tagen

Der regebenst Ge

Hinsicht sein ursprüngliches Ges

zuständigen Departements der k.k

k.k.Statthalterei abgegangen ist

das Gesuch solange vorläufig une

gefertigte das genaue Datum ange

Prag , am 25.S

kannt gegeben werden können.
tigte ändert also in dieser
, welches nach Mitteilung des
lizei-Direktion bereits an die
d bittet die k.k.Statthalterei,
digt zu lassen, bis der ergebens
kann.

ember 1916.

Dr Franz Kafka
Prag Poříč 7

newspapers. The members of the committee were tried in June 1911, Borek being sentenced to ten months' hard labour with bread and water once a month.

The club was one of the smaller radical societies, especially as compared with Augustin Smetana's Society of Freethinkers, which held a protest meeting attended by some 2,000 people on the occasion of the execution of the Spanish free-thinker Francisco Ferrer. As the danger of belonging to it increased, the club's membership grew even smaller, dwindling from 158 in 1902 to only 21 just before its suppression. The members were all young people, mostly workers and craftsmen, and under Borek's leadership looked for guidance to anarchist centres abroad, especially in Paris, as was shown by material seized during house searches. The police regarded the club as the 'Prague anarchist headquarters'.

Kafka is not listed among its members, nor does his name figure in the police reports of its meetings or the judicial interrogations of its officials, thorough as they were. This does not prove, of course, that he was not an occasional, unobtrusive participant; but if he had attended meetings at all regularly the fact could hardly have escaped notice and we should certainly find a record of it in his police dossier. The only name similar to his in the list of anarchists is that of Anton Kafka or Kavka, born at Sedlice, a teacher by profession and a writer of occasional verses.

Kafka's police record, in fact, contains nothing adverse or out of the ordinary. In noting this we should bear in mind the pedantic thoroughness of the Austrian police. If anyone committed the slightest misdemeanour and had to pay a fine, or if his dog got lost or he attracted attention in any other way, he was certain to figure in the police archives for the rest of his life.

Kafka was in fact twice investigated by the police. The first occasion was when he began his year of court work in 1906, prior to which he had to apply to police headquarters 'for a certificate of good conduct for the purpose of entering the service of the State.' On this occasion the police completed the application form with data concerning his parents, brothers and sisters, and of Kafka himself they wrote: 'unmarried, of Jewish faith and good behaviour'. An annexed sheet bears a stamp with the all-important inscription, to be found repeatedly in the dossiers of those who have at no time been involved adversely with the police: 'No ground for objection'. Before affixing this stamp, enquiries were always made by telegraphing to other police offices that might be concerned. A month

Document on p. 107: personal description of Kafka, in connection with a passport application.

Jméno / Name	*František Kafka*
Zaměstnání / Beschäftig.	*JUDr. – vicesekretář úraz. poj. děl.*
Rodiště / Geburtsort	*Praha*
Obec domovská / Zust. Gemeinde	*"*
Bydliště / Wohnort	*Staroměst. nám. 6.*

Popis osoby — Persons-Beschreibung

Narozen / Geboren	*1883 3/7*	Ústa / Mund	*3*
Postava / Gestalt	*nadprostř.*	Nos / Nase	*3*
Obličej / Gesicht	*oblg*	Zvl. znamení / Bes. Kennzeichen	
Vlasy / Haare	*černé*	Náboženství / Religion	*katol. mos*
Oči / Augen	*hn. m. š.*	Stav / Stand	*svob.*
Rodiče / Eltern	*Něm:*		*liter. Vorlesung*
Cíl cesty / Ziel der Reise			
Doba platnosti / Giltigkeitsdauer	*28/11 16.*		

...cestující — Mitreisende

Narozen roku / Gebertsjahr	Stupeň příbuzenství / Verwandschafts-Verhältnis	Poznámka / Anmerkung

later, on October 5, 1906, the police investigated Kafka once more, this time at the request of the district court, with the same result. The process was repeated on October 30, 1907 when he took up his job with the Assicurazioni Generali, and again at the end of May 1910 (soon before the suppression of the Young People's Club), when Kafka and four of his colleagues were being taken on to the permanent establishment of the Workers' Insurance Office. In October 1911 he once more obtained a police certificate of good conduct on the occasion of becoming a partner, in his brother-in-law's stead, in a concern trading in asbestos. This was a period of great activity on the part of socialist, atheistic and anti-militaristic societies like those of Augustin Smetana and Vilém Körber, in which the writers of memoirs would have us believe that Kafka took part.

Document on pp. 109–15: Kafka's passport, issued by the Imperial and Royal police authorities at Prague.

This is not, however, the end of the documentary material about him in police archives. In January 1915—after the first breach with Felice, when he was beginning once again to think of marriage with her as a refuge—he submitted an application for a passport. As it was wartime and he was liable to be called up, though not for armed service, he needed special permission to go abroad. We have a draft of his application, full of erasures testifying to his difficulty in phrasing it; it reads: 'Dr. Franz Kafka, assistant secretary in the Workers' Insurance Office for the Kingdom of Bohemia, proposes to undertake a journey of two days' duration, on January 23 and 24 of the current year, in order to visit in Berlin his fiancée [sic] Felice Bauer, daughter of the late Karl Bauer, commercial traveller, and his wife Anna Bauer, resident at Wilmersdorfer Strasse 73, Berlin W. The applicant is not liable to active service, so that no breach of military regulations would be occasioned by his crossing the frontier. The application is accordingly hereby submitted for approval.' It was in fact approved, but Kafka never collected the travel permit, although invited to do so three times at quarterly intervals. Instead, he met Felice on January 23 and 24 at Podmokly (Bodenbach) in Bohemia. The police archives contain several travel applications by Kafka and also passports surrendered by him at different times. We thus find the record of a journey to Hungary in 1915 with his sister, who was visiting her husband in the army. From the fall of 1916 there is an application, with attached documents, for permission to travel to Munich, where on November 10 he read his story *The Penal Colony* to an audience, including Felice, in the Goltz art gallery. The application runs: 'The undersigned Franz Kafka, doctor of laws, and assistant

The world is opening up, yet we humans are driven along narrow defiles of paper work. All we can be sure of is the chair we are sitting on. We live by rule and line, yet in fact each of us is a maze. A writing-desk is a bed of Procrustes; but we are not ancient heroes, and so the torture makes us no more than tragi-comical.

Diese Photogr ___ ___ stellt ^{dem} Passinhaber

Herrⁿ **Franz Kafka**

dar, ^{die}selbe hat ^{seine} Unterschrift eigenhändig

vollzogen. Der k. k. Regierungsrat
und Leiter der Polizeidirektion:

(16 Seiten enthaltend.)

Nr. 106657
R. P. 12.775

Im Namen Seiner Majestät

Franz Joseph I.

Kaisers von Oesterreich, Königs von Böhmen
u. s. w. und Apostolischen Königs von Ungarn.

Reise-Paß

für Herrn Franz Kafka

Charakter *Vizesekretär der Arbeiter-Unfall-*
Beschäftigung *Versicherungsanstalt für das*
Königreich Böhmen in Prag

wohnhaft zu
Prinzlich:
im Bezirke

Prag Böhmen

Kronland

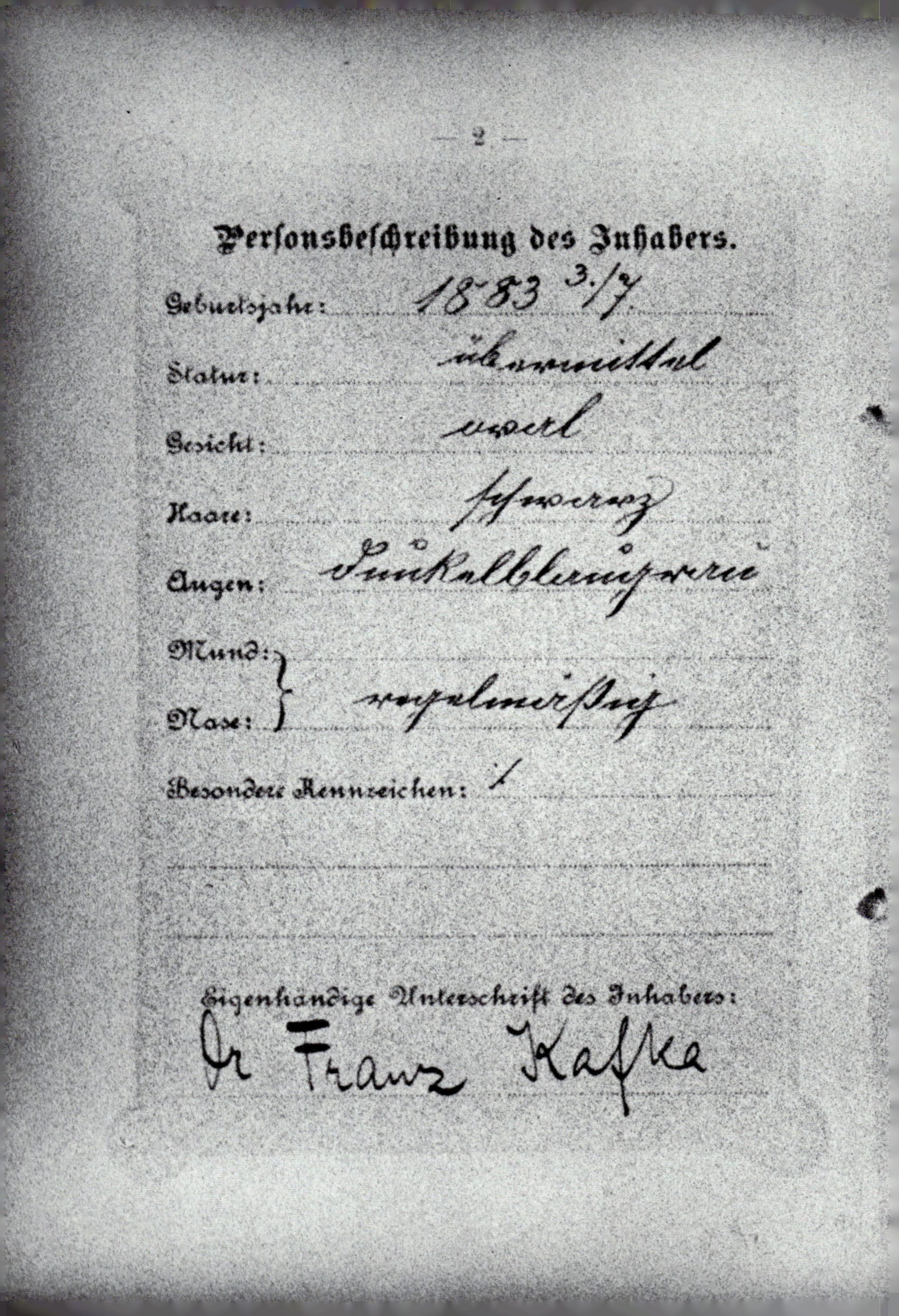

Personsbeschreibung des Inhabers.

Geburtsjahr: _1883 3/7_

Statur: _übermittel_

Gesicht: _oval_

Haare: _schwarz_

Augen: _dunkelblaugrau_

Mund: ⎫
⎬ _regelmäßig_
Nase: ⎭

Besondere Kennzeichen: _/_

Eigenhändige Unterschrift des Inhabers:

Dr Franz Kafka

in der öster.-ungar.

Dieselbe reist
Monarchie u. Deutschland.

Reisezweck: Liter. Vorlesung

Dieser Pass ist giltig:

Bis 28. November 1916

Prag, am 23. Oktober 19 16

Im Namen Sr. Excellenz des k. k. Statthalters:

der k. k. Regierungsrat und Leiter

der Polizeidirektion:

Mit Euch ▨▨▨ reist:

Namen und Vornamen	Charakter	Geburtsort	Alter	Stand	Statur	Ge-sicht	Haare	Augen

— b —

J.-Nr. 1340? Gen. Tarif Nr. ...

Gut zur einmaligen Reise:

von Prag

über Eger

nach München

zum Aufenthalt in München

Reisezweck Literarische Nach-
forschungen

und zurück über Eger

in der Zeit vom 4. November 1916

bis zum 16. November 1916

Prag, den 4. November 1916.

Der Kaiserlich Deutsche Generalkonsul.

Kühn

Hofrat.

KAISERLICH DEUTSCHES GENERALKONSULAT IN PRAG

secretary in the Workers' Insurance Office for the Kingdom of Bohemia in Prague, resident at No. 6, Altstädter Ring and officially domiciled in Prague, born in Prague on July 3, 1883, hereby applies for the issue of a passport in order to visit Munich, valid for the period October 5–7 or 10–12, 1916. In support of this application he submits the following documents and information:

'1. A letter dated September 12, 1916 from the art gallery "Neue Kunst Hans Goltz in München", inviting the undersigned to take part on October 6 or 10 in a series of lectures organized by that gallery.

'2. A pamphlet entitled "New Literary Evenings", containing fuller information about the lectures in question.

'3. In the conscription of June 21, 1916 the undersigned was declared fit for armed service with the *Landsturm* and assigned to the joint forces of the Crown. As certified by the attached copy of Decree No. 27333, dated June 23, 1915, issued by the Presidium of the Imperial and Royal Governor's Office for Bohemia, the undersigned is exempted from *Landsturm* service for an indefinite period.

'4. A certificate of domicile is appended.

'The necessary photographs will be furnished subsequently.' The date of the lecture was afterwards changed, and Kafka had to submit a fresh application. However, the police noted on the above: 'The applicant can be regarded as reliable and of good character. He is apparently subject to call-up on October 10, so that there would seem to be no objection to granting the application for a very short period, since there is no reason to fear any infringement of military or other regulations.' Various confirmatory notes and signatures follow, including the indication 'No objection on the part of the State police', signed by the Inspector Slavícek who broke up the Young People's Club and specialized in combating anarchists and other subversive elements; dozens of other reports attest the excellence of this zealous official's memory.

Kafka crossed the frontier at Cheb on November 10, 1916 and reported next day to the police at Munich; he also obtained from the city authorities coupons for a fortnight's supply of bread, meat, eggs, milk, butter, potatoes, cheese, sugar and soap. On November 12 he returned to Bohemia via Cheb.

Another document of the same kind is an application to travel to Hungary on 'family business' in June 1917; Felice accompanied him and they visited her sister at Arad. The police stamp again bears Slavícek's signature.

An important contribution to Kafka's biography is supplied by

Documents on pp. 117 and 118: application, in Czech, for a certificate of good conduct to enable Kafka to become a partner in his brother-in-law's asbestos works.

Slavné

C. k. policejní ředitelství

v

Praze

Žádám zdvořile za laskavé vyhotovení vysvědčení Zachovalosti za účelem tím, jelikož míním se státi společníkem továrního jednatele.

Děkuje předem, znamenám

Ph. Dr. František Kafka

Zaměstnání: úředník,
Rok narození: 1883
Byt: Praha ... Mikulášská tř. 36.
Obec domovská: Praha.

JUDr František Kafka

V Praze, XVI Mikulášská třída
č. 36, žádá za vysvědčení
zachovalosti.

Priora: 102333 ai 02 und
3741 ai 1906. ———

Opatřen listem domovským
z Praha 19/4 1906 č. 422 jako
dotud, r. 1883 roz.

Sproštěn za Děpán na čím
ovratě v červnu 1906.

Svoboden, potřebuje vysvěd-
čka vůli oprovození živnosti
ko společník tovarního podniku.

Telegr. č. 1894

Venkovské komisarství

ční-li tam závady proti
JUDru Františku Kafkovi,
83 roz., do Prahy příst.?
I. II. 27/10 11.

Rano, dne 27/X 1911

Venkovních komisarství proti JUDr
Františku Kafkovi, není žádné
závady
Na o dne 28/X 911

Vysvědčení.

C.k. policejní ředitelstv
stvrzuje, že na pana
JUDra Františka Kafk
úředníka
roku 1883 rozeného,
Prahy
příslušného, v Praze I
Mikulášská třída č. 36 bytem,
zde dosud nic nihonné
na jevo nevyšlo.

Vysvědčení toto vydá-
vá se K vůli oprovození
živnosti jako společníka
tovarního podniku.

V Praze, dne 28/10 190

Mdt. 29/X. Haužvic.—

Vid Exspedit peto Vrusenov
ního Ins. L. K. Vlamryule

a set of documents of October 1918. On the 9th, four weeks before the armistice with Austria-Hungary, the State Office of the Kingdom of Bohemia for the Welfare of Returning Servicemen wrote as follows to police headquarters in Prague:

'In connection with recommendations for honours in respect of welfare services for disabled members of the armed forces, we request that you include among those deserving such recognition Dr. Franz Kafka, assistant secretary in the Workers' Insurance Office for the Kingdom of Bohemia.

'Since 1915 Dr. Kafka has been responsible for preparing the agenda of the Committee for Therapeutic Treatment and supervising the execution of its decisions, in addition to his similar responsibility in the field of insurance. He deals with correspondence concerning the establishment and administration of sanatoria, and is particularly concerned with the State sanatorium for nervous diseases of ex-servicemen at Frankenstein.'

Frankenstein is a suburb of Rumburg (Rumburk): its Czech name is Podhájí, and the sanatorium is there to this day. Kafka made official trips to Rumburg, especially in the summer and autumn of 1918, evidently in connection with its affairs. The *Letters to F. B.*, recently published, contain the text of an appeal drafted by him on behalf of the German Association in Prague for the Establishment and Maintenance of a Military and Civilian Sanatorium for Nervous Diseases in German Bohemia, inviting the German community to contribute to the project for the benefit of ex-servicemen. By June 1916 the number of those requiring treatment in Bohemia is said to have been about 4,000. The appeal, which is German-nationalistic in tone, states that the decision to found the sanatorium was taken in October 1916 at an assembly in Prague of representatives of the community throughout Bohemia. It describes methods of assisting in the Association's work and is signed by over a hundred prominent citizens of German race, including Kafka and his chief Robert Marschner on behalf of the Insurance Office. In a letter of October 30, 1916 Kafka mentioned it to F. B. as follows: 'You will see my name among the signatories: I was originally to have been in the Preparatory Committee listed at the top, but was able without much difficulty to transfer myself to the large group at the bottom. The text, like so many others, is my handiwork.'

These and similar activities caused Kafka to be recommended for an Austrian decoration. In the twelfth hour of the monarchy's existence the official machine was still working with precision and promptitude, as though the awarding of decorations was to go on for at least another hundred years. On October

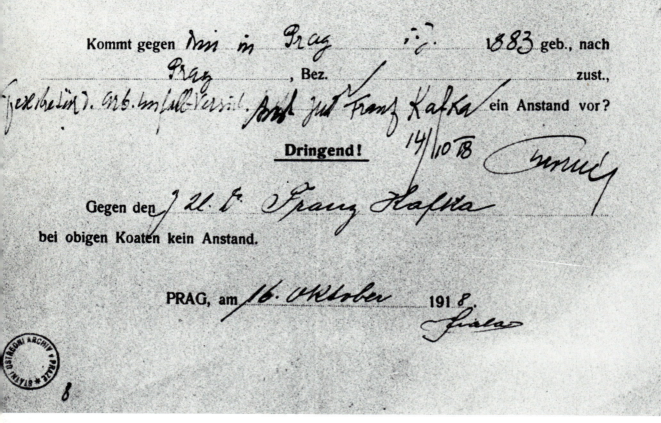

Documents on pp. 120 and 121: enquiries made by the Prague police in connection with Kafka's application for a certificate of good conduct.

12, 1918 the commissar of police for the Altstadt annotated the recommendation: 'Lives with his father at 16 Altstädter Ring; is unmarried, at present suffering from influenza. Nothing to his moral or political detriment is known at this office.' On the 22nd—six days before the proclamation of Czechoslovak independence—the recommendation was forwarded to police headquarters with endorsements by the local offices concerned. It was still being dealt with on the 26th, and it would have been a truly Kafkaesque touch if the decoration had been solemnly conferred on the day when Austria-Hungary ceased to exist. However, there is only one further note on the police dossier; it is in Czech and reads: 'In view of the latest events this is inoperative and can be filed away.' The note was typed on October 31 with a German machine, the Czech accents being added in pencil.

Several documents in the Prague archives deal with Kafka's journeys abroad for treatment in foreign sanatoria, especially Merano, which was now Italian territory. The applications are signed with the Czech form of his name 'Dr. Frantisek Kafka' and accompanied by various documents such as a 'foreign currency declaration', a printed form with the impressive text: 'I hereby solemnly declare that I have in my possession no

$\frac{12.287}{1918.}$

$\frac{K}{7}$
$\frac{}{13.}$ $\frac{1586}{}$ _M_ $\frac{K}{11}$
$\frac{}{23}$
_m._

$\frac{K}{42}$
$\frac{}{6.}$

Kommt nicht vor!
26. X. 1918

Následkem událostí posledních dnů
budiž co bezpředmětné

založeno.

31./10.1918.

foreign exchange, securities, gold or silver coins or bullion'—clearly the Czechoslovak bureaucracy was already worthy of its Austrian heritage. From the abundant stamps and signatures it is sometimes possible to ascertain dates that have hitherto been missing in his biography. In many cases he was unable to collect the permits himself and Ottla or his mother did so for him. The documents also provide the information that he was enrolled in the Twenty-eighth Infantry Regiment.

After many journeys to Austria, Germany and Italy came the last journey of all. In March 1924, when Kafka was in Berlin, his health took a sharp turn for the worse. In the middle of March he was brought back to Prague, and his family applied for a passport valid for several countries, as they were not sure where he would next go for treatment. On March 28, in a hand showing signs of illness, Kafka wrote to the passport section of police headquarters: 'I hereby authorize my mother to collect my passport as I am unable to do so personally.' Her receipt for it was signed on the following day. At the beginning of April he was taken to Vienna.

On March 29, 1934, ten years after Kafka's death, the military records section of the Prague municipality wrote as follows to police headquarters: 'We should be obliged if you would insert a notice in the police gazette to enable us to issue a certificate of discharge to Frantisek Kavka [sic], present address unknown, a lawyer by profession, born August 3, 1883, legally resident in Prague, son of Herman and (mother's first name unknown)... Last known address Prague III, house No. 365 in Land Registry. Kindly inform us of the results of your enquiries.'

The police duly enquired and ascertained that Kafka was registered at the above address from March 2, 1917 onwards; later the file is minuted: 'Is he still living at No. 6, Staroměstské náměstí?' (i.e. the Altstädter Ring)... Thus, ten years after his death, when the first edition of his works is in preparation and the first monographs are being written about him, Franz Kafka is still being sought by the authorities in order that they may issue to him his discharge from military service. It would be hard to find a more Kafkaesque instance of the bureaucratic machine at cross-purposes with the individual.

Documents on pp. 123 and 124: recto and verso of an extract from the file on Kafka dated 1934, showing that the Prague military authorities were trying to trace his whereabouts ten years after his death.

Magistrát hlavního města Prahy

Referát vojenský .

Č.j.VII ‒201974   29 III 1934

V Praze ....

                                                   F ‒‒‒‒‒‒‒

                        Policejnímu ředitelství

                                           v   P r a z e .

            Žádáme za laskavé uveřejnění v policejním
oznamovateli za účelem *stavení promeškacího lhůta* hledaného
.... Kafky Františka , právníka ....
nar... 3/I 1883 ... do ... Prahy .. příslušného, ...
rodičů .... Hermana .... a ...... (nezjevné.) .....
roz.......................
            Poslední jeho bydliště ... Praha III ...
č.p. 365 ...
            Výsledek pátrání budiž nám sdělen.

                        Za primátora :

        1/ Výpravno: Dr. Piček
                   Magistrátu hlav. města Prahy
                        referátu vojenskému

            K tamnímu dožádání ze dne 29.3.1934 č.j.VII 20197/4
sděluji,že jmenovaný zemřel v jistém senatoriu u Vídně dne 3.VII.1933
pochován jest však v Praze.Matka zemřelého Julie Kafková bydlí v Praze
Bílkové ul. č.4.
VYPRAV...
18.IV. 1934 2/ Odděl.IV.
‒‒‒‒‒‒‒ na vědomí.
                                   Kom. Dr. ......

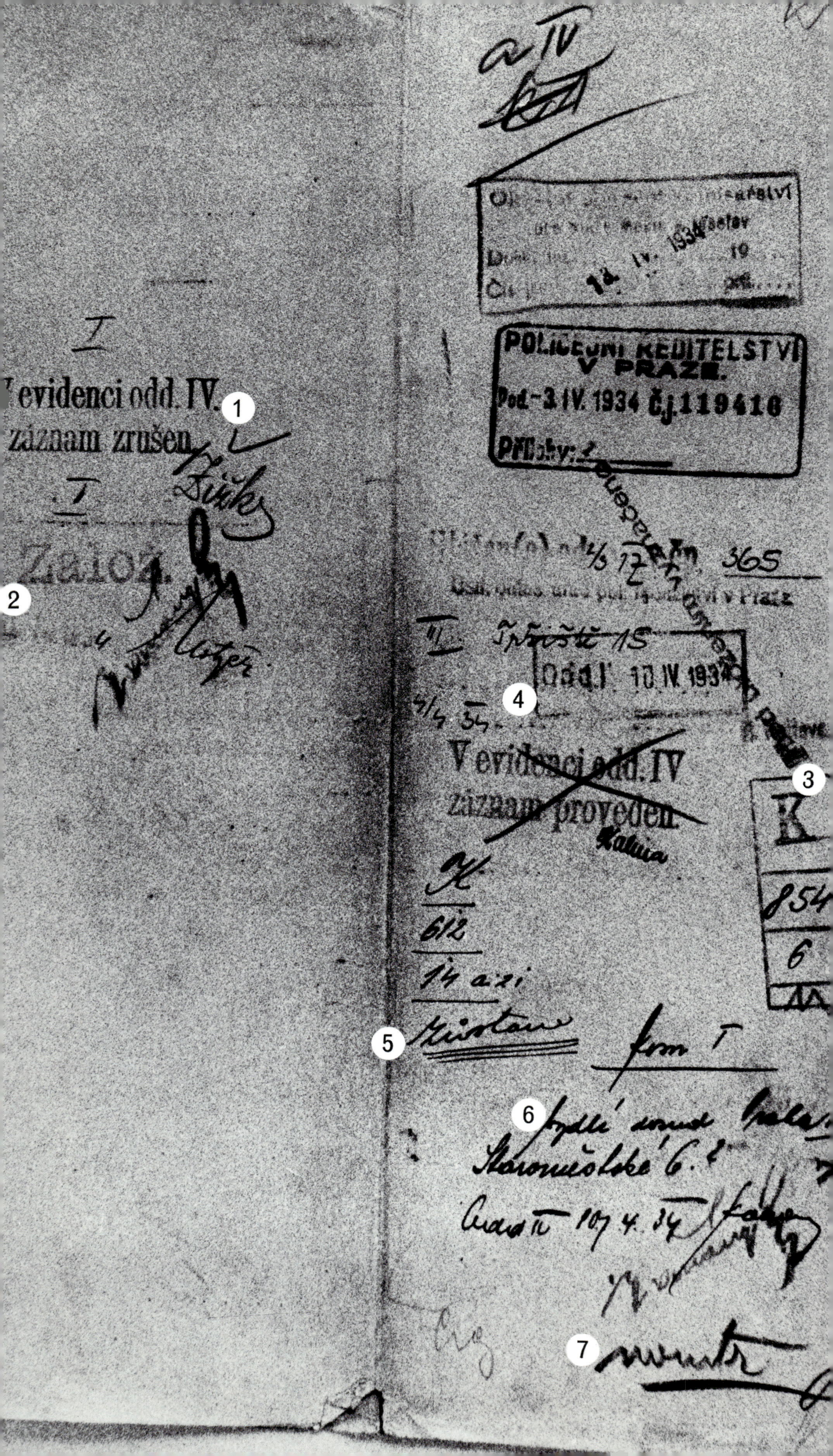

I

V evidenci odd. IV.

záznam zrušen

I

Založ.

POLICEJNÍ ŘEDITELSTVÍ
V PRAZE.
Pod. 3. IV. 1934 Č. j. 119410
Přílohy: 2

365

II. Křišté 15

Odd. I. 10. IV. 1934

V evidenci odd. IV
záznam proveden.

K
854
6

612

14 a zi

Staroměstské 6.

10. 4. 34

Notes on the document reproduced on page 124

1 In the files of Section IV
  Notice cancelled

2 To be filed

3 Noted before filing

4 In the files of Section IV
  Noted

5 K
  612
  14 and 21
  remains

6 Still resident in Prague I,
  Altstädter Ring 6?

7 Inside.

Kafka's sister Ottla, nine years younger than he, was the only member of his family with whom he was on terms of confidence.

To be sure, nothing is easy to bear, and happiness itself—even the most real kind of happiness, a ray of light, a stroke of lightning, an order from a higher power—is a formidable burden. But this is not a topic for letters, this is something 'for the bathroom'.

eat, bed at eleven, a well-heated room—meanwhile she resets my watch to the exact minute, whereas for the past three months I have kept it an hour and a half fast.'

In 1916 they spent their holiday together at Marienbad and agreed on practical arrangements for the future. The war made it difficult for them to meet, as there were restrictions on crossing the international frontier. At the end of 1916 Kafka accepted an invitation to give a public reading in Munich, and they were able to meet there.

At this time Kafka was finding himself more and more shut out from the world. His family, his office work and Prague all seemed to him threatening and restrictive. To Prague he ascribed all the negative features of the 'world' from which he had detached himself; he felt he had lost his fight with the city, and expressed a longing to live in Berlin. Felice was his only tenuous link with reality. Other attempts at contact, such as the absurd idea of getting himself drafted for active service, must be interpreted as a desperate rebellion against a state of affairs that threatened to become permanent.

Kafka's family was involved in his struggle over marriage with F.B., and among them he found a single ally in his youngest sister Ottla. Their relationship grew closer as the years went on, as is shown by a collection of letters found some years ago in Prague. Franz became his sister's counsellor especially at the time when she was set on deciding her own fate in opposition to her father—she was the only one of the family who could stand up to him openly. The conspiratorial meetings between Franz and Ottla were held in the bathroom. In Franz's own case, his desire for independence existed side by side with a sense of belonging to the family; the two were interdependent, and the result of their conflict was always in doubt.

'What I wrote about troubles wasn't, of course, meant quite seriously—sensible people have no troubles and the other sort of people are never rid of them—but when you are away from home your relationship to everything there becomes quite different—you no longer see the dangerous details, so you feel exceptionally powerful and clear-sighted. You feel as though, if she had any sort of trouble, you could dispel it at a single stroke from where you are; and that is why, for the sake of my own power and not because of your troubles, I wanted you to write and tell me of them.'

'Here [at Schelesen] it is fine too and very warm: it is nearly evening, but I am sitting on the veranda without a rug and I had my midday meal in the sunshine with the window open. Outside, underneath the window, are the dogs Meta and Rolf,

who waited for me to appear on high with the remains of my dinner, like people in the Altstädter Ring waiting for the Apostles [when the clock strikes the hour].'

'Incidentally, the word "but" written in on top is rather interesting: like writing in pencil, it is obviously an imitation of your ways, just as I used to find expressions in your letters that repeated themselves noticeably from one to the next and, although they were quite good German, nevertheless sounded unusual and almost artificial, especially when thus repeated—they did not express what they were meant to, yet they rested on a perfectly sound basis had one only known what it was. Actually I only realized when reading your letter before last that they must be translations from Czech, and accurate ones too (not like Father the other day telling Mr. D. in Czech that he was "on the friendliest foot" with someone or other), but for some reason the German language refuses to adopt them, at least as far as I, being only half a German, can judge.'

In the summer of 1914, when he was thirty-one years old, Kafka left his family, not by his own desire, and lived in a succession of rented homes, which he changed frequently. They were all in picturesque districts: the Waldhausergasse and the Lange Gasse in the Old City, the Alchimistengasse in the Hradschin quarter (near the Royal castle) and finally an apartment in the Schönborn Palace in the Malá Strana. It was here that the vomiting of blood took place which told him of his illness. The little house in the Alchimistengasse was put at his disposal by Ottla to work in the afternoons and evenings; it was actually built into the Castle wall and had formed part of the guards' quarters—not those of Rudolf II's alchemists, as legend has it. It consisted of a single room, opening directly on to the lane.

'Yesterday evening there was another row, a short but a violent one. The same old subjects: Zürau; the crazy girl, deserting her old parents; what sort of work can you get there now?; easy enough to live in the country when everything is plentiful; just wait till she's short of food and has real troubles, etc.★ This, of course, was all aimed indirectly at me, and from time to time I was openly accused of being to blame for such ab-

---

★ I should add, to be fair, that nice things were said about you too (implying envy of me): a girl "as steady as a rock", and so forth.

Milena Jesenská, the 'great love' in Kafka's life.

Because I love you (and I do love you, you obtuse creature, as the sea loves a tiny pebble lost in its depths, just so my love covers you with its waves—and may the heavens grant that I become a pebble in your depths too), for this reason I love the whole world, including your left shoulder—no, it was the right one first, and I shall kiss it whenever I want to and whenever you are so kind as to slip the blouse off it, and your left shoulder and your face bending over me in the forest and your face below me in the forest and my resting on your half-naked breast. And so you are right when you say that we have been united, and of this I feel no fear—it is my only happiness and the source of all my pride, and I am by no means thinking only of the forest.

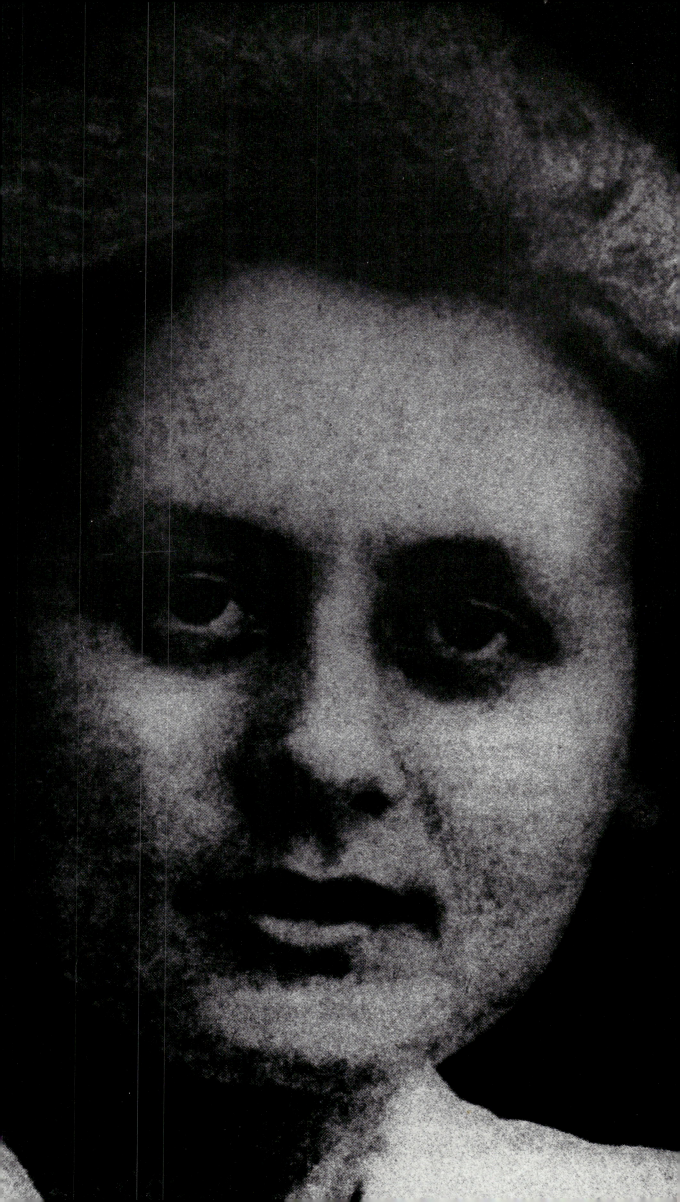

abnormal behaviour, at least abetting it—to which I made the pertinent or at any rate effective retort that there were worse things than being abnormal, for instance the war was a "normal" phenomenon.'

'After you left there was a great windstorm in the Hirschgraben, whether by chance or design I don't know. I spent last night in the Palace; when I went up to the house [in the Alchimistengasse], the fire had gone out and it was very cold. So that's it, I thought to myself—the first evening without her and I'm done for already. But then I got hold of all the newspapers I could, and some manuscripts, and before long I got a very decent fire going. When I told Ruzenka about it she said I ought to have chopped some kindling-wood, that was the way to get a fire going quickly. I replied craftily "But there isn't a knife there," to which she innocently answered "I always use the dinner knife." That explains why the knife is always dirty and why its edge is spoiled, but at any rate I've learned about making firewood.'

'So I've moved. Closing the windows in my place in the Palace for the last time, bolting the door—how very like this it must be when one dies. And now, in my new life, I feel a touch of headache for the first time since that morning of blood. Your bedroom isn't the kind one can get any sleep in. I have no complaint to make of the kitchen or the courtyard, it's noisy there by 6.30 in the morning but that's natural, even though today is a Sunday. Not even the cat was to be heard, only the clock in the kitchen. But the bathroom—! I counted three times when the light was turned on there and water was run for unknown purposes, and then the door to the other bedroom was left open so that I could hear Father coughing. Poor Father, poor Mother, poor Franz.'

In July 1917 Kafka became engaged to Felice for the second time, after which they went on a visit to her sister in Hungary. A few days after their return the illness declared itself—tuberculosis of the lung, which had been awaiting the moment to strike and which from now on thwarted everything that offered any hope for Kafka's future, his livelihood and above all his relations with Felice Bauer.

Kafka's struggle for F.B. was the greatest venture in his life, and it was a failure. A chance meeting led to this fight for the unattainable, for a victory over the world in and through Felice, who in his eyes represented that world in its better aspect. The termination of his relationship with her, and the onset of the disease which was to take control of his life, mark the beginning of his final battle—a battle no longer fought on two fronts, but within and against himself, and one which continued literally as long as he had strength to fight.

'For the rest, let me tell you a secret which must be true although at this moment I do not believe it myself: I am not going to get well. This is not a kind of tuberculosis that you cure by lying in a deck-chair, but a weapon pointed against me which must exist as long as I live—and we cannot both exist together.'

After his final parting with Felice at the end of 1917 Kafka stayed for some time longer with Ottla at Zürau in western Bohemia, some 60 miles from Prague; his subsequent life was divided between the Insurance Office, sanatoria and summer resorts. His illness at first appeared as a kindly relief, and only by degrees did he discover the depths of its malignity.

In 1919, at Schelesen near Liboch, about 25 miles northwest of Prague, he met a Czech Jewess named Julie Vohryzek, the daughter of a semi-proletarian shoemaker and synagogue attendant in the Prague suburb of Králové Vinohrady. They spent six weeks together in the sanatorium, their acquaintance developing in the hothouse-atmosphere of disease. In summer they became engaged, and the wedding was fixed for November; a one-room apartment was found in Vrsovice, a purely Czech part of Prague. In this way Kafka would have moved from the city centre to a Czech milieu, which would have given him the shelter of anonymity. We know scarcely anything of Julie herself, and we should know very little about the relationship if it were not for a long letter which Kafka wrote to her sister after the breach with her and which was recently published by Klaus Wagenbach. The sudden development of the affair and its equally sudden end for no discoverable reason suggest that it was of critical importance: Kafka was once again grasping desperately for a world to which he was already alien. 'It was I and I alone who pressed for marriage—I deliberately destroyed a life that had been full of peace.' The affair met with opposition from Kafka's father, to whom Julie was anything but a desirable match. As for Kafka himself, all his old misgivings about marriage broke out. 'You who have to fight unceasingly for your own existence, putting forward all your strength and finding that it is not enough—how can you think of trying to found a family, which may be the most elementary thing in life but is anyhow the most decisive and the boldest?' As a government official he belonged, as he put it, to the 'dregs of the European professional class'; and there he was, 'a man with weak lungs, a bundle of nerves, engulfed in all the perils of literature and wearily shirking the petty routine of the office.' The letter to Julie's sister shows the same outlook as the well-known one to his father, which was written at about the same time and from similar surroundings. 'The matter went through several phases. First the medical examination was delayed because the professor was on holiday—that was bad; Then my father tried to stop us, though not for too long; his opposition was a good thing, since it diverted my thoughts from the real dangers. Then we found that a reasonable home was to be had right away—so it was all worked out, just a short hurried week to go, the banns were arranged and we would have been married. Then suddenly on Friday it turned out that we couldn't have the apartment and therefore couldn't marry on Sunday. I won't say it was a misfortune—there might have been a worse crash later on which would have engulfed both of us. All I do mean to say is that my hope of marrying was not baseless and that the facts show me to have been a poor man and therefore the plaything of chance, but not a liar.'

In the first half of 1920 Kafka became acquainted with another Czech (not a Jewess), Milena Jesenská. She was twelve years younger than he, the daughter of a university professor of medicine. One of her ancestors was Jan Jessenius, the rector of Prague University who was executed with other Czech leaders, after his tongue was cut out, on the Old City square after the battle of the White Mountain. Milena, however, had broken with her family and lived what was in those days a life of scandalous independence. She finished her schooling at Minerva, the girls' Gymnasium in the Wassergasse, and with her emancipated friends formed the first group of Czech female intellectuals with a highschool education. Apart from love of the open air, travel and sport, she and her companions were distinguished by bobbed or shingled hair, a contempt for the rules and conventions of good behaviour, eccentric ideas of adventure (such as swimming across the Vltava at night), a gypsy-like taste in dress and furniture, a habit of expressing their feelings without restraint and the determination to live life sensually and to the full. Kafka met Milena briefly in a Prague café, but their real contact began early in 1920, when she was translating some of his stories (the first was *The Stoker*) for Czech magazines: these were in fact the first translations of his work. She was living in Vienna as a journalist and was married to Ernst Polak, though their attachment was a loose one. Kafka was afraid of the meeting and postponed it, but when they did see each other for four days in Vienna he experienced a sense of relief and pleasure. The love affair was mainly an epistolary

Dora Dymant, Kafka's companion at the close of his life.

one. A crisis took place after a one-day meeting at Gmünd on the Czechoslovak-Austrian frontier, and their liaison succumbed to a series of obstacles; Milena in any case could not bring herself to divorce Polak. From distant sanatoria Kafka wrote insisting that they break off relations.

'Do not write and do not let us meet again—this is my only request and I beg you to fulfil it in silence. Only so can I go on living—anything else would destroy me still further.'

Kafka showed his trust in Milena by confiding to her his Diary and some manuscripts. She loved him as no other woman had done: the vehemence of her feeling was expressed in the letters she wrote at the time of losing him, which Max Brod described as 'a wild cry of despair'. Few of their contacts took place in Prague, as Kafka spent most of this period in sanatoria, vainly seeking deliverance or at least a postponement of his fate.

During a stay on the Baltic coast, where he was taken by his eldest sister when seriously ill, he made the acquaintance of Dora Dymant, a Polish Jewess who worked in the 'Jüdisches Volksheim' in Berlin and who thenceforward shared the little life that remained to him. 'It would have been quite impossible for me to live alone in Berlin, or indeed anywhere else, but at Müritz I found an unexpected remedy for this also.' Thus in the grim period of the German inflation, when he had not enough to eat despite frequent parcels from Prague, and when the shadow of his illness fell more and more heavily, he found a relationship of human affection that was terminated only by his death.

Kafka regarded it as the greatest happiness in life to marry and beget children. For many years women represented a refuge from the frustrations of the world and the circle that was closing around him, when his profession, his family and his friends were unable to afford him the support he needed. Marriage with Felice Bauer was the object of his most desperate struggle, but it was doomed to failure: she, like other women, belonged to the world from which Kafka was separated by an ever-widening abyss. His later attempts were a vain endeavour to recapture the irretrievable. As a result, writing came to bear the brunt of his struggle against the world, his ever-frustrated attempts to break out of isolation. Till the very end of his life, on this uncertain ground, he fought the contest with undiminished vigour. Hope of help from outside was gone. The help that he could gain from literary work, as a more or less genuine substitute for real life, was in some respects a deliverance, in others a diabolic deceit.

VIII   ILLNESS AND DEATH

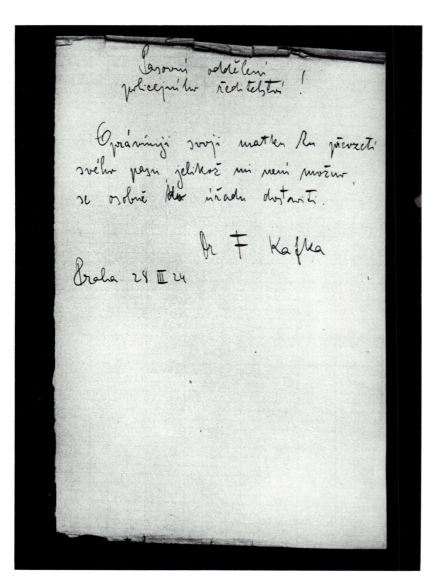

Documents on pp. 152 and 153: Julie Kafka obtained the necessary papers for her son's last journey abroad.
'To the Passport Department, Police Headquarters: I hereby authorize my mother to collect my passport as I am unable to do so personally. Dr. F. Kafka.'

From 1917 onwards, the steady deterioration of Kafka's health was the decisive factor affecting all aspects of his life. In earlier years he had complained of weakness and exhaustion, but had put them down partly to the insomnia which always troubled him and partly to the strain of alternating, or 'manœuvring' as he called it, between the life of an office clerk and that of a literary artist. As he wrote in 1916 in a letter to the publisher Kurt Wolff: 'For the past three or four years I have played ducks and drakes with my life (in the most honourable way possible, which makes things much worse), and now I am enduring the painful consequences... All I can do now is wait until the only remedies likely to be of any use are within my reach, namely a bit of travel and plenty of rest and freedom.' Nevertheless the onset of the disease in 1917 took Kafka by surprise. It occurred at the beginning of August, and took the form of blood-spitting and vomiting on two consecutive nights. Kafka was apparently not over-alarmed, but that he was aware of tuberculosis as a possibility is clear from a letter he wrote three weeks later to his sister Ottla:

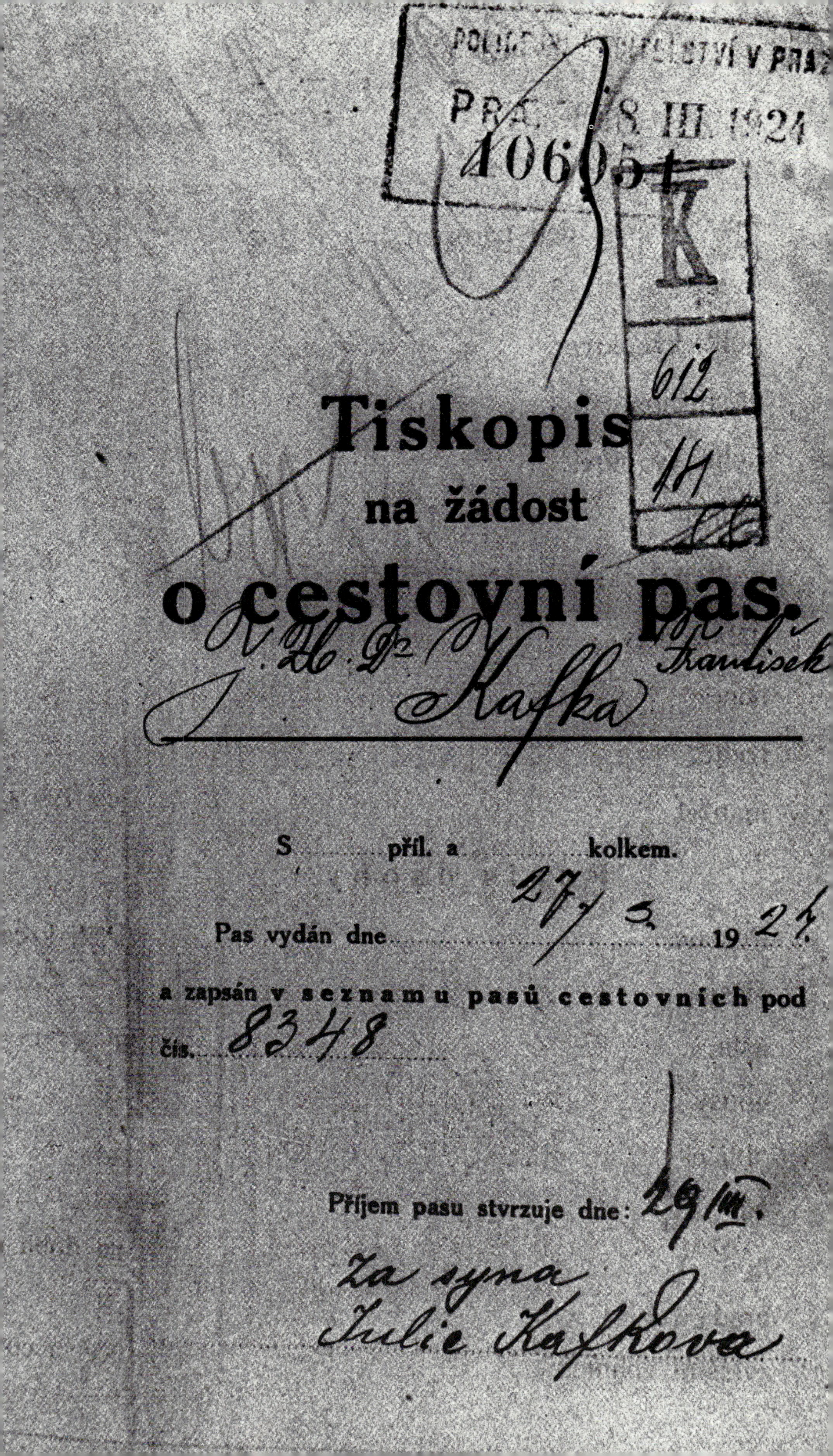

K

612

14

Tiskopis
na žádost
o cestovní pas.

V. 26. Dr. Kafka František

S............. příl. a .... kolkem.

Pas vydán dne.............................. 27/ 3. 19 24

a zapsán v seznamu pasů cestovních pod

čís. 8348

Příjem pasu stvrzuje dne: 29/III.

za syna

Julie Kafková

For the rest, let me tell you a secret which must be true although at this moment I do not believe it myself: I am not going to get well. This is not the kind of tuberculosis that you cure by lying in a deck-chair, but a weapon pointed against me which must exist as long as I live—and we cannot both exist together.

Only then my thoughts merged in one another, for the Moldau and the part of the city on the other side are wrapped in the same darkness. . . A few lights on the far side played tricks with the beholder.
Description of a Struggle

I walked forlornly along the Ferdinandstrasse.
Diaries

And thus help goes away again, having helped in nothing.
Conversations

'About three weeks ago, during the night, I had a hemorrhage of the lung. It was about 4 o'clock: I awoke, wondered why my mouth was watering so much, spat it out and turned on the light—strange, it was a patch of blood. Then I really began to vomit—*chrlení*, I don't know if that's how you spell it, but it's a very good expression for the way it wells and bubbles up in your throat. I thought it would never stop—how could I stop it, I hadn't turned it on in the first place. I got out of bed and walked about the room, went to the window and looked out, came back again—still nothing but blood, then at last it was over and I went back to bed and slept better than I had for a long time. Next day (an office day) I saw Dr. Mühlstein: he talked about bronchial catarrh and prescribed a medicine, told me to take three bottles of it and come back in a month, or immediately if the bleeding started again. Next night I vomited blood again, but less. Back to the doctor—I hadn't thought much of him in the first place. I won't go into the details, it would be too much altogether. It seems there are three hypotheses. *Firstly* a severe cold—the doctor says so, but I don't believe him. I never catch colds, how could I do so in August? —though it's true the apartment might have something to do with it, being chilly and ill-smelling. *Secondly* consumption: the doctor won't admit this for the present but doesn't rule it out either, according to him all city-dwellers are tubercular. Meanwhile he talks about 'catarrh of the apex of the lung' ('apex' is nice and cosy, like speaking of a piglet when you mean a sow)

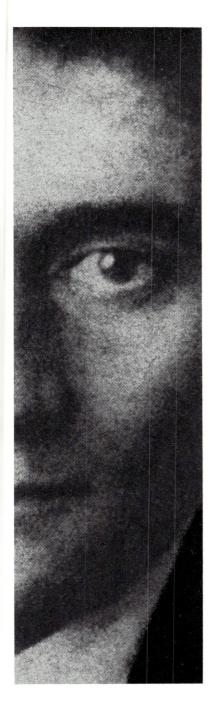

and says there is nothing so frightful about this, you inject tuberculin and it's cured. *Thirdly*—of course I only hinted at this, and he wouldn't hear of it. But it's the only real possibility, and fits in perfectly well with the second. The old, crazy illusion had been plaguing me of late, in fact last winter was the longest intermission in the last five years of suffering. It is the greatest battle with which I have ever been afflicted, or entrusted rather, and a victory—which might for instance take the form of marriage, perhaps F. is only a symbol of what may be called the good principle in this struggle—a victory, with no more loss of blood than can be endured, would have been a Napoleonic event in my private and cosmic history. But now it looks as if I am being defeated in precisely this way.'

Throughout his life Kafka was suspicious of medical diagnoses, and it was all his friend Max Brod could do to get him to visit a specialist. He did so on September 4, 1917; the doctor diagnosed catarrh of the apex of the lung and prescribed three months' holiday. A further examination revealed double tuberculosis. Kafka thereupon took his first extended leave from the Insurance Office and spent eight months in Zürau (Sírem) in northwest Bohemia, where his sister Ottla was looking after a farm belonging to her brother-in-law. Here he hoped to find the 'rest and freedom' that were so painfully lacking in Prague.

During these months in the peace of the countryside he continued to reflect on the origin of his illness on the lines indicated in his letter to Ottla. The illness became part of his struggle with the world; it was a stigma which he had to bear, but at the same time it became his ally, not least in the relationship with Felice Bauer. She came to see him at Zürau in the middle of September; three months later, in Prague, they broke off relations, thus ending 'five years of sorrow' and the hardest struggle of his life. Was Kafka's illness the real reason for their separation? 'Sometimes,' he wrote, 'I feel as if my brain and my lungs had conspired without my knowledge. My brain must have said: "This cannot go on," and now, after five years, my lungs have agreed to do their part.' We shall doubtless never know for certain how far his illness may have been due to psychological causes, but we do know that at the beginning he regarded it as 'almost a godsend', as he indicated in several letters to his friend Felix Weltsch:

'So the illness in its initial stages seems to me more like a guardian angel than a devil. But I dare say that the way it develops will be the devilish part, and that in retrospect what I think of as angelic will prove to be the worst of all.' 'You are

quite right, of course—in order to recover one must have the will to do so. This I have, but, if it is not "precious" to say so, I also have the will not to. It is a curious illness, a kind of special dispensation, quite different from anything else I have ever had in this line. I feel like a lover when he says: "Everything before this was an illusion, I am in love for the first time."'

But this ambivalent attitude towards a disease which he also looked on as a punishment never degenerated into hypochondria. After his stay in Zürau he returned to Prague, but for the next few years was obliged to spend recurrent periods in sanatoria. At first he was strongly opposed to the idea of going to a lung sanatorium for treatment, but eventually he had to consent to this. He stayed twice in Schelesen in 1918 and 1919, and in Merano in the spring of 1920; then in December 1920 he went for a nine months' cure to a small private sanatorium in Matliary in the High Tatras. There he met a young medical student, Robert Klopstock, who was himself consumptive and was working at the sanatorium as a nurse. The friendship that developed was initially based on their common interest in Hebrew and in Jewish philosophy, but developed into a warm human relationship. Apart from Dora Dymant, Klopstock was Kafka's only constant companion in the last period of his life. He succeeded, as long as Kafka was at Matliary, in distracting his friend from the besetting problem of his illness, so that Brod, who attempted several times to find out how the cure was progressing, had to draw up a questionnaire in order to get satisfactory answers. Kafka filled in the blanks in his usual ironical style:

Gain in weight?	17½ pounds.
Present weight?	Over 143 pounds.
State of lungs?	Doctor's secret, but said to be satisfactory.
Any temperature?	Not as a rule.
Breathing?	Not good, on cold evenings it's almost like winter.
Signature	This one really stumps me.

The cure was in fact not so successful as these answers might suggest. Kafka returned to Prague without having really recovered his strength.

In 1922 he left Prague twice more for short stays at Spindlermühle (Spindlerův Mlýn) in the Giant Mountains and Planá nad Luznicí in southern Bohemia, where he was again looked after by Ottla. Before leaving for Planá he took steps to be

Pictures on pp. 162–9: The Jewish cemetery at Strasnice, Prague, where Kafka was buried on June 11, 1924.

Hluboce zarmouceni podáváme zprávu, že náš syn

JUDr. František Kafka,

zemřel dne 3. června t. r. v sanatoriu Kierling u Vídně, jsa stár 41 roků. Pohřben bude ve středu, dne 11. června t. r. o. ³/₄ hod. odpol. na israel. hřbitově ve Strašnicích.

V PRAZE, dne 10. června 1924.

Heřman a **Julie Kafkovi,**

24229   jménem veškerého příbuzenstva.

Kondolenční návštěvy se s díky odmítají.

In tiefstem Schmerz geben wir bekannt, daß unser Sohn

JUDr. Franz Kafka

am 3. Juni im Sanatorium Kierling bei Wien, 41 Jahre alt, gestorben ist. Das Begräbnis findet am Mittwoch, den 11. Juni um ³/₄ Uhr auf dem jüdischen Friedhof in Straschnitz statt.

PRAG, am 10. Juni 1924.

Hermann und **Julie Kafka,**
Eltern,

8392   im Namen der trauernden Hinterbliebenen.

Von Kondolenzbesuchen bitten wir abzusehen.

finally pensioned off by the Insurance Office; for despite the advanced state of his illness, his superiors were reluctant to agree to this. He wrote to Ottla:

'So I broached the matter today, naturally to the accompaniment of some sentimental play-acting, without which I can never part from anyone. Instead of just demanding to be retired (this would be mendacious too, but it would at least be honest at a certain level), I started to talk about not wanting to abuse the Office's confidence etc. Naturally the upshot is that they are quite determined not to retire me—perhaps they wouldn't have agreed to in any case. As for leave, I shall certainly get that, though I can't see the Director till Monday and don't know yet what he thinks. The Professor's medical report —it is little different, if at all, from what he told me, but things change when they are written down—is for all the world like a passport to eternity.'

'I saw the Director today. I don't think I shall ever manage to leave the Office, except by favour of galloping tuberculosis.'

His application for retirement was finally granted at the end of June 1922.

In July 1923 he went with his sister Elli to Müritz on the Baltic coast, where he met the nineteen-year-old Dora Dymant. She

The presentiment of an eventual liberation is not made
invalid if on the following day the captivity remains
unchanged or is even made harsher or even if there is
a clear statement that it will never end. All this can,
in fact, be the necessary condition for the eventual
liberation.

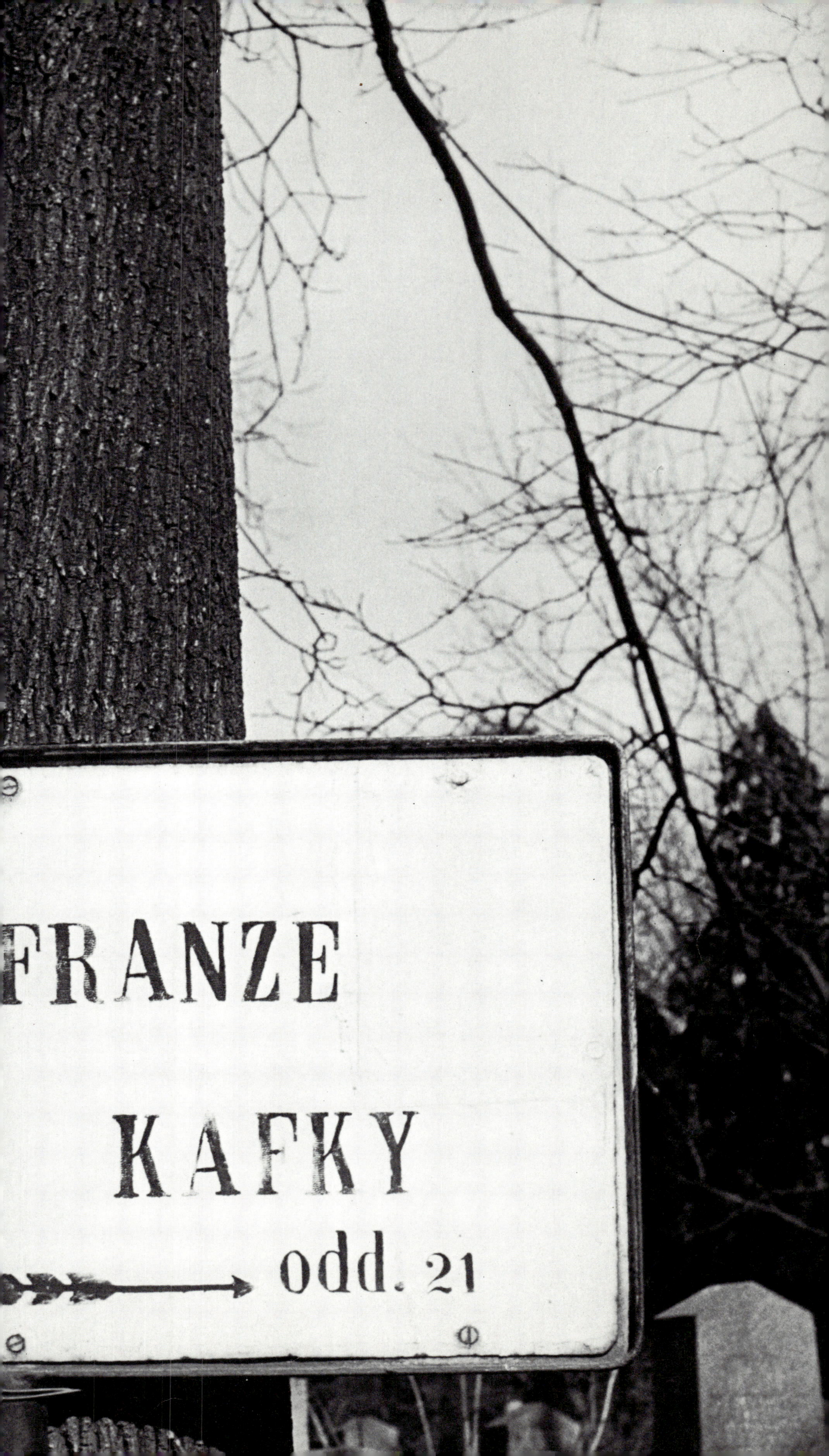
FRANZE
KAFKY
odd. 21

showed towards him the understanding that he had sought from women all his life, and was his companion during the months that remained to him. In September 1923 he succeeded in carrying out his intention of leaving Prague in order to set up an independent existence with Dora Dymant in Berlin. As far as his health permitted, he felt relatively happy in the German capital, but this did not last long: the winter of 1923/4, with currency inflation and the resulting deprivations, accelerated his illness unmercifully. Dora Dymant wrote: 'It was the time of the inflation, and Kafka suffered severely. Every trip to town was like a Way of the Cross for him—physically he almost collapsed. He would queue for hours on end, not in order to buy anything but because he felt that among people whose blood was still flowing, his would flow too.' In March 1924 his uncle Siegfried and Max Brod brought him back to Prague. The remaining stages of his *via dolorosa* followed quickly: the Wienerwald sanatorium, the University Clinic in Vienna, where the treatment did not suit him, and finally Dr. Hoffmann's sanatorium in Kierling near Klosterneuburg. Here his condition got rapidly worse, so that he could neither speak nor eat nor drink. His tuberculosis had spread to the larynx, and an operation was now out of the question. To spare his parents distress he refused to let them visit him. The last tragic hours by his bedside were shared by Robert Klopstock and Dora Dymant, whom he no longer recognized owing to the effect of morphine. His last words were an expression of concern for a fellow being: seeing Klopstock bending over him, he believed that it was his sister Elli and, fearful lest she catch the infection, he exclaimed: 'Don't come so near, Elli, not so near... There, that's better.' He died on June 3, 1924 and was buried a week later in the Strasnice cemetery in Prague, the city whose 'claws' had never let him go.

I expect I shall last another week—perhaps—I hope—there are such nuances.

Each limb as tired as a whole human being.

The lilac is wonderful, isn't it?—even when dying it drinks, like a fish you might say.

Even if it cicatrizes—I apologize for these revolting questions, but you are my doctor, after all—it would take a matter of years, and all that time one would be unable to eat without pain.

There was a bird in the room.

Is it possible for the pain to stop occasionally? I mean, for any considerable time?

Put your hand on my forehead for a moment, it will make me braver.

Whoever heard of a dying man drinking?

To want death but not pain is a bad sign. Still, for the rest one is prepared to face death. As in the Bible, the dove has been sent forth; but it has failed to find an olive leaf, so it slips back for the present into the darkness of the ark.

IX KAFKA AND THE CZECHS

This tremendous universe that I have in my head—but how can I free myself and set it free without being torn to pieces? Yet I would a thousand times rather do that than keep it confined or buried within myself. This is what I am here for, I have no doubt whatsoever of that.

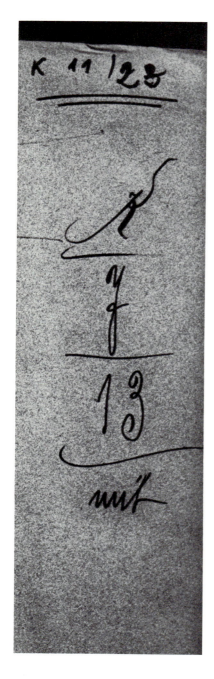

Prague meant more to Kafka than his native city usually means to a poet or an artist. To a large extent, it was the background against which his whole relationship to the world was formed. While he was still young the city was both familiar and promising; it was part of his intimate being, and its threatening aspects were mere contingencies of secondary importance. As the years went on, however, Prague too became a symbol of impotence, a part of that external world from which Kafka was shut out and with which he lost touch. While he was young he sought, hopefully and with all his strength, to achieve contact with the city and its inhabitants, both on his own account and with friends. When the circle of incomprehension closed around him, he turned in on himself or looked far beyond Prague to Berlin or Palestine, involved in either case with dreams that had as little reality as those of a bedridden invalid.

The city is to be found in his works as well as in his life. Not, to be sure, in its panoramic aspects: the image of these is dull and incomplete, though in his early work and especially in *Beschreibung eines Kampfes* it is clearer than later on. It has become a hobby of literary historians to find references to scenes or places, but the true image of Prague in Kafka's writing is a deeper one. It is to be found in the stream of its language and the vision of the lonely genius who lived his life in the ancient city centre and, from that narrow base, constructed an imaginary picture out of real elements. The language and attitudes, the situations, incidents and humour of Kafka's stories would all be unthinkable without the Prague background from which they spring.

For those who know and love him, Prague is first and foremost the city of Franz Kafka. When they walk about its streets they are amidst his books, and when they read his books they feel as if they were treading the city's streets and squares, with their narrow passages and balconied houses. The mysterious works that have baffled so many analyses, the distinctive life and unreality of Kafka's Prague background have become a fertile soil for legend among Jews, Germans and Czechs alike.

To the world of Czech culture, Kafka has always been close at hand yet at the same time remote. It has never been able to take him for granted as something native and indisputable. He always belonged to the intellectual underworld rather than to the light of day—an adept of artistic mysteries, of the great obscure issues of life and knowledge with which humanity contends, forever uncertain whether it is winning or losing the battle. Kafka in Bohemia was always the great unknown: a Wandering Jew and a haunter of crooked alleys, a poet whose

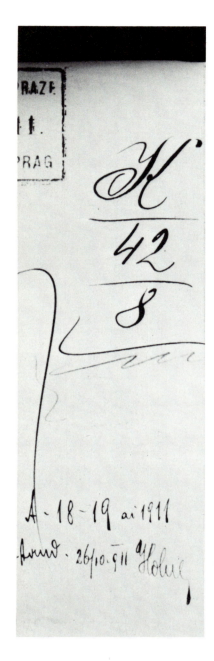

theme was the chaos and anxiety of civilization, a prophet of calamities to come.

The Czech literary world for the most part viewed Kafka with reserve, and even today his works are imperfectly known and appreciated in his own country. The first and much the most important interpreter of them to the Czech public was Milena Jesenská, who translated and published some of his shorter stories over a period of three years—the only translations to appear during his lifetime. In this way the circles which first became acquainted with his work were those of the left. In 1920 Stanislav Kostka Neumann devoted a whole issue of his review *Kmen* to Kafka's tale *The Stoker*, with a prefatory note describing it as one of the best examples of modern German fiction. Neumann also wrote an obituary of Kafka for the Prague *Communist Review*, in which he said: 'This writer with the gentle soul saw deeply into present-day social injustice; he loved his exploited fellow men and, in obscure but penetrating language, mercilessly condemned the rich. Those comrades who were readers of *Cerven* [*sic*, a mistake for *Kmen*] will undoubtedly remember the impressive story of his that was published there.' Neumann intended to publish a whole book of Milena's translations, but the postwar shortage of paper and money made it impossible.

By and large, Kafka was scarcely known in the Czech community at the time of his death, and one of the three obituaries that appeared in the Czech press misspelt his name Kavka, like the word for a jackdaw. One of these articles stated that he had left two completed novels in manuscript form. In another, Jan Grmela wrote: 'On June 4, Franz Kafka died of a lung disease in an Austrian sanatorium. He was a German-language writer of rare quality, a pure and delicate soul who held our corrupt world in abhorrence and dissected it with the scalpel of his reason. He saw deeply into the social system, the poverty of some and the power and wealth of others, and in a style full of imagination and parody launched a fierce attack on the great ones of this world.'

The most eloquent farewell, however, was Milena Jesenská's in *Národní listy*:

'Franz Kafka, a German writer whose home was in Prague, died the day before yesterday in the Kierling sanatorium at Klosterneuburg near Vienna. He was little known among us, being a solitary and timid soul; for years he had suffered from a lung disease and, although he received treatment for it, it was a constant factor in his life and consciousness. "When one's mind and heart can carry the burden no longer, the lungs take

part of it upon themselves so that at least it may be more equitably borne": so he once wrote in a letter, and such was the nature of his own illness. To it he owed, in part at least, his extraordinary delicacy, intellectual refinement and fierce refusal to compromise, while, as a human being, he made his illness responsible for his intellectual fear of life. He was a shy, apprehensive man, kind and peaceable, yet his books were full of pain and cruelty. He saw the world as a place full of invisible demons waiting to rend and destroy defenceless human creatures. He was too wise and clear-sighted to cope with life: his weakness was that of fine and noble souls who are paralyzed by fear of misunderstanding, unkindness and intellectual dishonesty—they know in advance that they are powerless, and they yield in such a way as to shame the victors. He knew his fellow men as do those who are gifted with acute nervous sensibility, who in their isolation can judge an individual from a fleeting glimpse of his face. He knew the world in a strange, profound fashion; he himself was a strange, profound world. His works are the most significant in modern German literature: they are free from slogans, but they reflect the struggle of today's generation everywhere. They are bare, truthful and painful, so that even when the language is symbolic the content is naturalistic. They reflect the ironical and sensitive outlook of a man whose vision of the world was too clear to be borne and who therefore went to his death, refusing to take refuge, as others have done, in semi-conscious error, however intellectual and however noble.

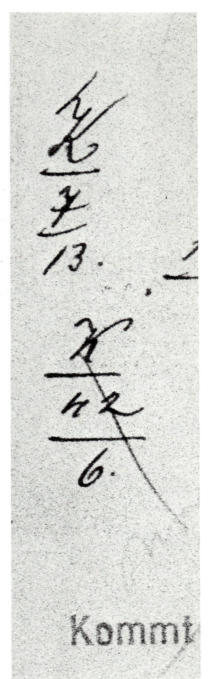

'Franz Kafka's writings include *The Stoker*, which appeared in Czech translation in S. Neumann's *Cerven*—the first chapter of a fine novel, still unpublished; *The Judgment*, depicting the breach between two generations; *Metamorphosis*, the strongest work in modern German literature; *The Penal Colony*; and also two sketches entitled *Meditation* and *A Country Doctor*. His last novel, *The Trial*, has for years been ready in manuscript and awaiting publication. These are books of the kind which leave the reader feeling that they describe the world so completely that nothing needs to be added. All his works are full of the sense of hidden misunderstanding, of human beings wronging one another without blame. Both as a man and as an artist his sensibility and anxiety were such that he perceived dangers when others, whose senses were duller, thought themselves safe.'

Milena's translations from Kafka came to an end in 1924, and she did not venture on any of the novels. An occasional reminiscence of his personality is to be found here and there

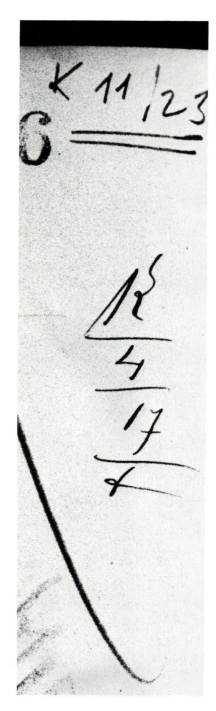

among her magazine writings, but it is usually of a vague and disguised character.

In the late twenties Czech interest in Kafka arose in a quite different quarter, this time of Catholic inspiration, thanks to Josef Florian, the creator of an independent publishing house at Stará Ríse in Moravia. Florian was originally a schoolteacher of natural history, but at the turn of the century he became acquainted with the work of Léon Bloy, which radically changed his life. He gave up teaching, retired to Moravia and, aloof from literary movements of all kinds, devoted himself in spite of material difficulties to publishing noteworthy books by out-of-the-way authors, many of whom, including Kafka, became known to the Czech public through his efforts. A stubborn individualist (he refused to send any of his eleven children to school and went to prison in consequence), he was constantly surrounded by people who became instruments of his plans and ideas. In Kafka's case there were three translators and a couple of German illustrators, Otto Coester and Albert Schamoni, who were roaming about Eastern Europe and stopped for a time with Florian, apparently for the pleasure of his company and for the sake of board and lodging. The first of the translators was Gustav Janouch, who later published *Gespräche mit Kafka* (Conversations with Kafka), which he apparently wrote while with Florian: he had known Kafka in Prague, and it may well have been he who brought him to Florian's notice It is curious that the most esoteric author of the twentieth century should, as far as Bohemia is concerned, have been the discovery of an amateur country publisher who had nothing whatsoever to do with literary schools and theories.

In the mid-thirties Kafka became known to the world at large. His collected works were published for the first time, though incompletely, and at the same time a biographical essay made its appearance. Reminiscences began to come from his contemporaries of the German-Jewish intelligentsia—with some tragic gaps in memory due to the lapse of ten years—and from people who had 'been to school with Kafka' and had been the first to know him as a person. The French surrealists, too, discovered him as an original literary source and an unacknowledged prophet of the modern age.

Some years before this concentration of interest, Kafka had been written about by Paul Eisner, a German-Czech writer, essayist and translator in Prague, who is certainly the best authority on Kafka's work to have appeared in Czechoslovakia. As far back as 1931 he spoke of the 'unique miracle of Franz Kafka' and prized his work above 'all the glories of the

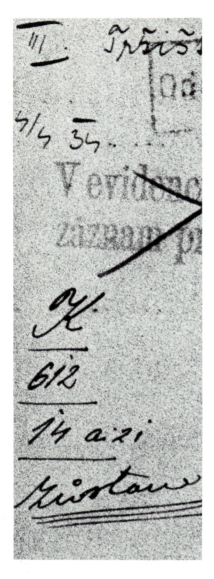

fiction of today. He also wrote pertinently of Kafka's 'scholasticism without revelation' and the 'metaphysical, commercial German strain', and attributed his work to a 'mixture of three races'. Eisner is the pioneer of the 'Prague school of interpretation' of Kafka's work, without *parti pris* or vulgarization. His Czech translation of Kafka's first novel, *The Castle*, appeared in 1935. The general public had not been prepared for it and did not understand it, so that it sold badly, but it had a powerful effect on writers, artists and intellectuals: it was in fact responsible for introducing a whole generation, those who read it at the impressionable age of twenty or so, to Kafka's peculiar brand of experience and awareness of life. The background to their impression was furnished by surrealism: in many cases Breton's *Index* pointed the way to the poet in whose steps they trod the streets of Prague. Meanwhile academic students of German literature in Czechoslovakia, whose interest in Kafka was much slighter at the time, classed him as an expressionist and interpreted his work accordingly.

Thus Kafka's definitive acceptance by Czech culture coincided with the peak of interest in surrealism, and the latter movement claimed him from the start as one of its forerunners. This determined the way in which he came to be understood by Czech writers and critics: as the revealer of secret processes that defeat human understanding, the discoverer of a new system of co-ordinates, cruel and grotesque in their effect and at variance with those of practical reason. He was thought of as the delineator of an alien world with its own precise yet inscrutable rules, the purpose of which is apparently to discredit our own world by involving it and us in a remorseless, unintelligible conflict. The confrontation of the two worlds results in basic and systematic misunderstanding—a 'witches' kitchen' for which the slang of Czech intellectuals has adopted the expression *kafkárna*.

By thus passing into the domain of colloquial speech and artistic mythology, Kafka in his own country transcends the immediate sphere of literature. He transcends, too, the city in which he struggled for the power to live and write, and becomes himself the exponent and the standard by which a whole world is judged.

And thus the circle along whose perimeter we move is almost closed. It is a circle
that belongs to us, but only in so far as we keep moving along it: the moment we
step aside in the slightest degree, through forgetfulness, absence of mind, fright,
astonishment, fatigue—at that moment the circle goes spinning off into space. Up
to now we have had our noses deep in the timestream—then we come up for air,
turn to walking instead of swimming, and we are lost. We are outside the law:
no-one knows this, and yet everyone treats us accordingly.

In Hebrew I am called Amschel
like my mother's
maternal grandfather,
whom my mother remembers
as a very devout and learned man
with a long white beard.
She was six years old when he died
and remembers
that she had to hold the toes of the corpse
and to ask to be forgiven for anything
she might have done to offend him.
She also remembers her grandfather's many books,
which filled the walls of his room.
Every day he bathed in the river,
and even in winter he would cut a hole in the ice.
My mother's mother
died early of typhoid.
From that day onwards
her grandmother became melancholy,
refused to eat,
spoke to no-one,
then, a year after her daughter's death,
she went for a walk and did not return . . .

Brief chronology

1883   Franz Kafka born (3 July) in the Old City in Prague, son of Hermann and Julie Kafka.

1889   German school on the Fleischmarkt.

1893   German Gymnasium on the Altstädter Ring.

1901   Graduates from the Gymnasium (July). In the autumn begins studying chemistry, and then law, at the German Karl-Ferdinand University in Prague.

1902   A semester of German studies. Journey to Munich (October). Resumes studying law in Prague. First meeting with Max Brod.

1902   Philosophy of Franz Brentano. Meetings in the Café Louvre.

1905   Acquaintance of Felix Weltsch and Oskar Baum. Writes *Beschreibung eines Kampfes* [Description of a Struggle].

1906   Receives doctorate of law. Takes up law practice (from October).

1907   Writes part of *Hochzeitsvorbereitungen auf dem Lande* [Wedding Preparations in the Country]. Temporary employment at the 'Assicurazioni Generali', an Italian insurance company (October).

1908   Accepts post at the Workers' Insurance Office in Prague (July).

1909   Publication of some prose in *Hyperion*. Trip with Max Brod to Riva and Brescia (September). Visit to the Young People's Club.

1910   Begins his Diary. Attends performances of a Yiddish theatre group. Trip to Paris (October).

1911   Vacation with Max and Otto Brod on the North Italian Lakes. Stays at the Erlenbach sanatorium, near Zürich.

1912   Begins work on *America*. Trip to Weimar (July). First meeting with Felice Bauer (13 August) and beginning of their correspondence. Writes *The Judgment*.

1913   *Meditation* published by Rowohlt (January). Trip to Vienna, Venice, Riva (September). Acquaintance with the "Swiss girl".

1914   Engagement to Felice Bauer (June). Engagement broken a month later. Works on *The Trial* and *The Penal Colony*. Acquaintance with Grete Bloch.

1915   Reunion with Felice Bauer (January). Takes room in Prague (initially in the Bilekgasse, then in the Langegasse). Trip to Hungary. Fontane Prize.

1916   Stays in Marienbad with Felice Bauer. Public reading

of *The Penal Colony* in Munich. Takes room in the Alchimistengasse (in the house of his sister, Ottla).

1917 Writes *A Country Doctor* stories. Takes room in Schönborn Palace in the Malá Strana. Second engagement to Felice Bauer (July). First symptoms of illness (diagnosed as tuberculosis on 4 September). Stays with Ottla in Zürau. Second engagement with Felice Bauer broken in Prague (December).

1918 Returns to office (summer). First meeting with Julie Vohryzková in Schelesen (November).

1919 Engagement to Julie Vohryzková. Writes *Brief an den Vater* in Schelesen (November).

1920 Sick leave in Merano. Begins correspondence with Milena Jesenská. Their first meeting in Vienna. Returns to Prague. Engagement broken. Cure from December in Matliary in the High Tatras. Beginning of friendship with Robert Klopstock. Writes various stories.

1921 Decline in health following his return to Prague in the autumn.

1922 Stays in Spindlermühle in the Giant Mountains. From June with Ottla in Planá nad Luznicí. Works on *The Castle*.

1923 In Müritz (July). Acquaintance with Dora Dymant. Moves to Steglitz, near Berlin (end of September). Writes collection of short stories, *A Hunger Artist*.

1924 Berlin. Returns to Prague (17 March). Admitted to the Wienerwald sanatorium (10 April). Following an examination in the University Clinic in Vienna, enters the sanatorium in Kierling. Dies 3 June. Buried 11 June in the Strasnice cemetery in Prague.

Works by Franz Kafka

America. Translated by Edwin Muir. New York, 1953.

The Castle. Translated by Willa and Edwin Muir, Eithne Wilkins and Ernst Kaiser. New York, 1954, and London.

The Trial. Translated by Willa and Edwin Muir and E. M. Butler. New York, 1957, and London.

Tagebücher [Diaries] 1910–1923. New York/Frankfurt am Main, 1951 (English translation, London, 1948–9 and 1964).

Description of a Struggle. Translated by Tania and James Stern. New York, 1958 (also contains other short pieces).

Wedding Preparations in the Country. Translated by Ernst Kaiser and Eithne Williams, in *Dearest Father*. New York, 1948.

Erzählungen [Short Stories]. New York/Frankfurt am Main, 1952.

Briefe [Letters] 1902–1924. New York/Frankfurt am Main, 1958 (some translated in London edition of diaries and letters, 1964).

Letters to Milena. Translated by Tania and James Stern. New York and London, 1953.

Biographies

Brod, Max: *Franz Kafka. Eine Biographie*, third edition. Frankfurt am Main, 1954. Translated by G. Humphreys Roberts and Richard Winston, New York, 1960.

Eisner, Pavel: *Franz Kafka and Prague*. New York, 1950.

Janouch, Gustav: *Gespräche mit Kafka*. Frankfurt am Main, 1951.

– *Franz Kafka und seine Welt. Eine Biographie*. Vienna/Stuttgart/Zürich, 1965.

Wagenbach, Klaus: *Franz Kafka. Eine Biographie seiner Jugend*. 1883–1912. Berne, 1958.

– *Franz Kafka in Selbstzeugnissen und Bilddokumenten*. Reinbek, 1964.

Index

Sources of quotations

Unless otherwise indicated, all references are to Kafka's collected works (*Gesammelte Werke*), edited by Max Brod, S. Fischer Verlag, Frankfurt, 1950. Page numbers in italics refer to quotations in the margin. The sources are abbreviated as follows:

B   Franz Kafka, *Briefe 1902–1924*

BF   Franz Kafka, *Briefe an Felice*

BM   Franz Kafka, *Briefe an Milena*

BO   Franz Kafka, *Briefe an Ottla* (unpublished)

BV   Franz Kafka, *Briefe an den Vater*

BR   Max Brod, *Über Franz Kafka*. Frankfurt, 1966

J   Gustav Janouch, *Gespräche mit Kafka*. Frankfurt, 1968

JB   Gustav Janouch, *Franz Kafka und seine Welt. Eine Bild-biographie*, Vienna, 1965

KS   Jürgen Born, Ludwig Dietz, Malcolm Pasley, Paul Raabe, Klaus Wagenbach, *Kafka Symposion*. Berlin, 1965

L   Jaromír Louzil, 'Dopisy Franza Kafky', *Review of the National Museum in Prague, VIII*. 1963

P   Franz Kafka, *Der Prozess*

T   Franz Kafka, *Tagebücher*

W   Klaus Wagenbach, *Franz Kafka. Eine Biographie seiner Jugend*. Berne, 1958

Page 7: B 14 / p.9: T 121 / p.14: T 418 / p.27: *BV 169* / p 30: J 116 / p.33: T 152f. / p.42: *BV 206f.* / p.45: BM 64f. / p.46: B 21f. / p.50: BV 167; *T 358* / p.53: BV 172f.; 181 / p. 60: BV 177 / p.62: BV 207f. / p.68: *P 220* / p.74: *J 105* / p.81: B 45; 37; 49 / p.82: B 48; B 55; 51; T 41 / p.84: *Br 76* / p.88: T 57f.; 78; 79; *J 163f.* / p.90: L 78 / p.81; W 173 / pp.94–5: *T 187; 141* / p.95: *J 153f.* / p.108: *J 137* / p. 128: T 283; 285; *BM 260* / p.130: BF 65ff.; 388; 390f. / p.132: BF 399; 407; 412f. / p.136: 425f.; 427; 443; 156f. / p. 139: BF 560; 584 / p.140: T 459 / p.141: BO / pp.144–6: BO; BO; BO; *BM 148f.* / p.149: Br 284; BM 268 / p.152: B 147 / p.154: *BF 757* / p.156: BO / p.157: B 161; 168 / p.160: B 180; 338 / p.161: BO; JB 159 / p.162: *T 541* / p.166; Br 185 / p.167; *B 484ff;* BM *235* / p.171: *T 219* / p.184: T 212f.